LOIS KELLY & CARMEN MEDINA

Rebels at Work

Dispatches

First published by GenreStar 2020

First edition

This book was professionally typeset on Reedsy.
Find out more at reedsy.com

Contents

III Communicating

IV Challenges & Obstacles

V Resilience for Rebels

VI Leading Rebels

Introduction

The world needs Rebels now more than ever before," we wrote ten years ago when we started researching and writing about Rebels at Work, the creative, smart, tenacious and purposeful people willing to rock the boat, challenge the status quo and move new ideas forward at work.

OK, we were wrong. The world REALLY needs all of us Rebels at Work now more than ever.

Over the past decade we've met thousands of self-identified Rebels at Work in all types of professions — including IT scrum masters, teachers, HR managers, librarians, doctors, nurses, government analysts, customer service reps, armed services officers, administrative assistants, social workers, labor union organizers, customer service reps, and curious senior executives. They've been from a huge range of industries, non-profits and government agencies, and from countries around the world.

These Rebels all share one trait: they care enough about their organizations to be willing to speak up and try to improve what no longer works or could work a whole lot better.

In meeting Rebels and hearing their stories, we've also learned a lot, fueling our quest to understand what effective Rebels do and how good leaders create conditions to support these most valuable employees.

With every experience, we each felt compelled to write blog posts about what we were observing and learning.

Our hope: help Rebels avoid mistakes, try useful, new tactics, and find the inspiration and self-awareness to become more resilient and keep on going despite obstacles and bureaucratic sinkholes.

We've taken ten years of those blog posts and experiences and distilled them into what we believe is the most important and useful advice for Rebels.

The content is practical, provocative, grounded in our real-world experience and the stories so many of you have shared with us, and served up with optimism, love, and occasional outrage. Whether you're starting out as a Rebel at Work, a seasoned veteran trying to overcome yet another obstacle, or a leader eager to empower her staff, there's something in this book for you.

We have concentrated on what we've learned since our 2014 book. Unlike that more traditional effort, these dispatches are quirky, representative of each of our personalities, and part of an ongoing understanding rather than a definitive, tidy formula for success. We tend to rebel against those who claim to be gurus and thought leaders, preferring to learn from adventurers who observe, experiment and adapt to constantly changing conditions.

Thank you for all you do in making your workplace more human, more meaningful, and much more likely to accomplish important goals.

Adelante!

Lois Kelly and Carmen Medina

I

Rebels: Know Yourself

Section Highlights: Rebels: Know Yourself

In any organization there are insiders, outsiders, and people who work at the edge of the inside. It is both a gift and a challenge to work at the edge of the inside, as most of us Rebels do.

In a memorable 2016 *New York Times* article, "At the Edge of the Inside," columnist David Brooks wrote:

> *"In any organization there are some people who serve at the core. These insiders are in the rooms when the decisions are made... Then there are outsiders. They throw missiles from beyond the walls... But there's also a third position in any organization: those who are at the edge of the inside. These people are within the organization, but they're not subsumed by the group think. They work at the boundaries, bridges and entranceways."*

Those of us who work at the edge of the inside can be the strongest reformers because we understand what's important to the organization and how it works — and we have the judgment of a critical outsider.

However, being on the edge of the inside can be really uncomfortable.

The insiders often get annoyed with us when we question the status quo, raise possibilities for doing things in new ways, or resist "going along" with policies and practices that no longer work. They may also dismiss our good ideas and challenge whether we are "team" players, eroding our confidence, credibility and commitment to doing good.

So while we need courage, which we explore in the Resiliency section of this book, we especially need self-awareness to thrive in our valuable role as organizational edge walkers.

In this section we look at how to get comfortable with this discomfort, channel our passionate and often intense energy in positive ways, reframe our value to the organization, and understand that change always takes much longer than we think it will.

Brooks based his essay on "The Eight Core Principles" by Franciscan priest Richard Rohr. One of those principles is: "Life is about discovering the right questions more than having the right answers."

Growing our self-awareness grows both our perspective and our ability to discover the right questions.

GET COMFORTABLE WITH DISCOMFORT

The Bearable Discomfort of Rebels

"The problem with Rebels at Work," my good friend and fellow rebel said, "is that it makes being a rebel seem very glamorous. And you know it doesn't seem very glamorous to me at all. In fact being a rebel is just a miserable thing and you're doing a disservice in your talks and writings by making it sound fun and easy."

Well, I've always known my friend to be very direct, but still his exposition pushed my back into the chair. I asked him if I could share his views, without attribution, and he agreed. Why without attribution? Because life as a rebel is hard and employers often don't appreciate rebel free speech.

Poor employers. Life isn't so easy for them either, even the ones who have good intentions. They're caught in what seems like an impossible dilemma. Most enlightened businesses want to be seen as places that empower staff and encourage different views. And yet the very last thing any traditional company wants is to be known as is the home of a growing rebel movement. The classic **DIYD/DIYD** problem.

So let this be a cautionary tale. Be warned that you will rarely feel comfortable in your work skin if you feel the rebel instincts stirring within you, and if you, as Umair Haque wrote in a blog post for HBR, care about doing deeds that:

- Stand the Test of Time
- Stand the Test of Excellence
- Stand the Test of You

(Umair Haque, by the way, refers to the above post as his "tiny statement of rebellion.")

An important sign of rebel maturity in the workplace is the realization that being an effective rebel, being true to yourself, means you will often feel uncomfortable at work.

Someone actually came up to me 15 years ago, seemingly out of the blue, to deliver this important piece of advice. I was at a business function and this woman, my memory is that she worked at DuPont, came up to me and said she could tell I was a heretic in my workplace. (Apparently I walk around with a vivid flashing neon sign atop my head.)

Her piece of advice: "You've got to learn to stop fighting this feeling of discomfort. You have to learn to accept discomfort as the indicator that you're being true to your beliefs." Short pause. "And you know it's not enough to accept the feeling of discomfort. You're going to have to enjoy feeling uncomfortable. You have to see the positive in it or you won't survive."

I confess I don't think I ever quite reached that higher level of enlightenment. But I always thought of that woman from DuPont as my guardian angel.

And, as I implied above, it's not easy being the manager of rebels either. Traditional management practices equate consensus with power and efficacy.

It is truly difficult, particularly as most managers have senior leaders above them judging their performance, to sustain an environment where individuals can speak freely and act meaningfully. A leader prepared to support the insurgency will also feel uncomfortable; but, as is the case with countries and nations, rebels often can't make a difference until they gain the support of at least one important legacy player.

Our hope is that Rebels at Work can start gathering the knowledge (and remember that knowledge includes both accomplishments and mistakes) that will help rebels be better rebels and give managers the tools and best practices they need to support ideas that matter.

Rebels do it together!

Jerry Garcia Was a Reluctant Rebel

There's a pervasive image of change makers as hell-bent, fire-breathing, go get 'em cowboy (or Steve Jobs) types of people.

Not really. Most of us are incredibly reluctant to get involved. Not because we don't care. But because we often feel that solving the problem requires expertise far beyond what we know. And because we know how HARD it is to change things inside a company, a non-profit, our children's school, or any organization that has been functioning a certain way for a while.

We keep thinking that the people with the expertise should see the problem and step in. But when it becomes clear that the people with the expertise aren't seeing the issue or acting, we feel that we must.

The fact is most rebels care too much to let a problem fester.

So we reluctantly get involved, even when we don't necessarily have the expertise to solve the problem.

When the late Jerry Garcia of the Grateful Dead got involved in efforts to save the rain forests he famously said:

> *"Somebody has to do something, and it's just incredibly pathetic it has to be us, with all the other citizens of the planet, and all the other resources out there, but since no one else is doing anything about it, we don't really have any choice."*

In a 1989 interview with High Times, Garcia explained his reluctance.

HT: You've made the statement that you think it's pretty pathetic that you're the ones who have to do it.

JG: Yeah, it is. It's an alarming feeling. This is an earth problem—the whole earth. And who's left talking about it? Us.

Come on! We're not the ones. We're not qualified to do it. But we're going to do it unless, or until, somebody else does. We're going to keep working on it. We're going to get as much support from as many people as we possibly can.

If we lose it (the rain forest), we're not going to get it back. It's definitely life threatening, in the same sense that atomic bombs are life threatening, only this one is mindless. It's gone along and there's nobody at the wheel. Out of control. Something needs to be done about it. We're alarmed—we're just making an effort to communicate our own alarm.

Rebel theme: "Something needs to be done about this. I guess I need to be the one to get things started."

If You're Not Part of the Problem...

Bill Torbert of Boston College once said to me that the 1960s slogan "If you're not part of the solution, you're part of the problem" actually misses the most important point about effecting change.

The slogan should be: **If you're not part of the problem, you can't be part of the solution.**

> *"If we cannot see how what we are doing or not doing is contributing to things being the way that they are, then logically we have no basis at all, zero leverage, to change the way things are — except from the outside, by persuasion or force."*
>
> *Adam Kahane, author of Solving Tough Problems: An Open Way of Talking, Listening and Creating New Realities*

Rebel Learnings

This summer I had an opportunity to talk to many rebel audiences. I know Lois did as well. And as usual we learned a ton from people we spoke with. So much is worth passing on. So let's get right to it.

The EGO

One of the groups I spoke to was the NextGen Leadership Summit in Washington D.C. It's a conference put on by GovLoop for civil servants at every level—federal, state, local.

Lois and/or I have spoken to the group several times now and I wish I could say that the situation for rebels in government has improved. From the questions I got, not much.

I was sharing our learning that for a rebel one of the best things that can happen is for someone else to take credit for their idea. In fact, we believe that a priority for all rebel change agents is to make your idea *their* idea.

Many participants didn't like my advice. At all! Getting any kind of personal recognition in their bureaucracy is so difficult. The idea of voluntarily eschewing it struck them as NUTS. After I spoke, a sympathetic person came up to me and said:

Carmen, to avoid this reaction, next time why don't you just say that rebels need to remember that it needs to be less about them and more about their idea. And leave it at that!

Admitting you're not perfect

Similarly, the NextGen audience balked at my suggestion that rebels avoid false confidence when presenting their ideas. You should admit that your idea is imperfect and invite others to make it better.

Again, many in the audience noted that the culture in their organization demanded confidence at all times. Acknowledging uncertainty is a cultural mistake and could even cost your group in that nutty competition for resources that occurs in so many bureaucracies. So you do have to calibrate how receptive your organization is to honest talk and how high its penchant for delusion. Maybe your candor can only occur in one-on-one or small group situations.

These next two ideas come from a conversation I had last month with Brice Challamel, a fellow rebel whom you can see in our learning video, *Be a Brave, Big-Hearted Rebel at Work.* He believes that an occupational hazard for Rebels at Work is the loss of perspective on their ideas. Rebels can do a better job at self-editing themselves with two simple tricks:

Develop some criteria to evaluate your ideas

For example, maybe you will only go forward with ideas that would benefit your immediate boss and improve conditions for other units in your organization, not just your own section. So as you sift the wacky ideas in your head, you have a basis for putting aside some and proceeding with others. And along those lines...

Limit the number of ideas

A real hazard for rebels is that they become known as flighty, jumping from one idea to another without ever seeing one through. Tell yourself that you can only advance two or three suggestions at a time. This then becomes another criteria by which to evaluate your thinking. It also will make you more effective by concentrating your energies and that of your supporters.

Whose Responsibility is Debbie's Mother?

Debbie's mother has called me 32 times over the past three days. She started calling on Monday night when the storm kicked in.

The Nor'easter wound down last night, not as bad as predicted. But Debbie's mother keeps calling. Six times this morning.

Debbie's mother has the wrong number. I am not Debbie.

I explained this fact to her during several calls. But still she called, thinking my number is her daughter's number. I looked up the incoming phone number and found that it was from Cedar Crest Nursing Home.

I called the nursing home to tell them that one of their patients (residents?) was upset and desperate to talk to Debbie. Could they please help her find the right telephone number for Debbie?

"I'm sorry. We have three floors of patients here. There's no way I can find the woman you're talking about," the Memory Loss floor supervisor told me. "Patients on my floor don't have access to phones so it's not one of mine. It must be someone on another floor. Sorry, I'm just too busy here."

"Could you make a call to your colleagues on the other floors?" I asked.

"I'll try," said the Memory Loss supervisor and then hung up.

Debbie's mother is trying to find Debbie. But Debbie's mother is lost inside the nursing home. There is no one to hear her, except for me, the wrong number.

How many are lost at work, calling and getting no response?

In my work with big companies I often feel that people are lost, calling those in positions of responsibility with ideas, cautions, and worries, and getting no response. They feel like Debbie's mother.

"I thought if I raised this issue, someone would be there to listen and do something about it," people think. "I thought this was the year we could finally start to make a dent in doing work that would make a difference. But I guess not."

After a while people stop calling, realizing that no one is going to pick up. They become complacent, doing as the floor supervisors request, yet worrying nonetheless.

We need people at work with the tenacity and hopefulness of Debbie's mother. Maybe this time the call will go through.

What we need more are floor supervisors who care as much about helping people in their company who are lost and searching as they do about maintaining order in their small organizational silos. What might happen if more managers truly cared about EVERYONE and not just "their employees" or their patients?

A rebel calling: taking responsibility

I have a lot to do today. But perhaps the most valuable thing I can do is to drive to the nursing home and find help for Debbie's mother.

In work and in life we rebels are often called to do things that we think someone else should be handling.

Responsibility is never neat and orderly.

My phone is ringing again. It's Debbie's mother.

CHANNEL INTENSE ENERGY

The Courageous (im)Patience of Rebels

Recently in the vast Twitter river, but so quickly that I do not remember details, I ran across a phrase attributed to Admiral Hyman Rickover:

> *"Good ideas are not adopted automatically. They must be driven into practice with courageous patience."*

COURAGEOUS PATIENCE. What a great phrase I thought and how it captures an essential virtue of rebels. COURAGEOUS PATIENCE.

Lois and I have written frequently about optimum rebel tactics. We have learned from many of our rebel profiles that perseverance and persistence are key rebel traits. Great rebels never surrender their visions to the bureaucratic swarm. We may suffer setbacks but we bide our time waiting for our opportunities, preparing for them.

Not all rebels, of course, believe in biding their time. Many launch themselves into frontal assaults against the bureaucratic landscape, usually without fully understanding the pitfalls that lie ahead. They stumble; some fall. Many observers think these individuals are the courageous ones, brave enough to take the establishment head on. And in many respects they are.

So who was Admiral Hyman Rickover? I imagine most of you under 50 have no idea who he was. The one sentence biography is that Rickover was the father of the nuclear navy. Soon after the development of nuclear power, Rickover came to understand what it could mean for the Navy, but most Navy thinkers did not agree with him. As the Wikipedia article notes:

> *Rickover's vision was not initially shared by his immediate superiors: he was recalled from Oak Ridge, and assigned "advisory duties" with an office in an abandoned ladies room in the Navy Building. He subsequently went around several layers of superior officers, and in 1947 went directly to the Chief of Naval Operations, Fleet Admiral Chester Nimitz, by chance also a former submariner. Nimitz immediately understood the potential of nuclear propulsion and recommended the project to the Secretary of the Navy, John L. Sullivan, whose endorsement to build the world's first nuclear-powered vessel, USS Nautilus (SSN-571), later caused Rickover to state that Sullivan was "the true father of the Nuclear Navy."*

And now for the really odd part.

What I also learned from researching the Rickover story is that the quote attributed to him, COURAGEOUS PATIENCE, is a misquote. He actually said exactly the opposite.

> *"Good ideas are not adopted automatically. They must be driven into practice with courageous* ***impatience****."*

Check it out for yourselves. Internet Quote sites have the Rickover line one way, the way I prefer it honestly and think is most provocative, but if you visit the US Navy's virtual museum, you learn presumably Rickover's correct insight.

So which is it then? Do good ideas need courageous patience or impatience?

I suspect the reason the quote is so corrupted is that both statements are true. The passion of rebels drives many to want to act immediately; they are impatient for others to see what they see. Others choose to wait, looking for their best opportunity to advance. They evince patience and the courage of self-control.

Quote confusion aside, Admiral Rickover's life story captures the complexity of most rebel stories. Govleaders.org has an excellent summary of his leadership principles in his own words. I particularly like this paragraph below, which describes quite accurately how the worldwide conspiracy for the preservation of mediocrity actually works.

> *A major flaw in our system of government, and even in industry, is the latitude allowed to do less than is necessary. Too often officials are willing to accept and adapt to situations they know to be wrong. The tendency is to downplay problems instead of actively trying to correct them.*
>
> *Recognizing this, many subordinates give up, contain their views within themselves, and wait for others to take action. When this happens, the manager is deprived of the experience and ideas of subordinates who generally are more knowledgeable than he in their particular areas.*

Adelante!

Keep the Channel Open

Agnes DeMille was talking to fellow dancer and choreographer Martha Graham in 1943, worrying that her recent success with *Oklahoma!* was unwarranted. DeMille wanted her work to be great, but questioned whether she could live up to her hopes.

The story goes that the generous and genius Martha Graham turned quietly to DeMille gave her this advice. Advice that perhaps all we innovators, rebels and passionate professionals should take to heart.

> *There is a vitality, a life force, an energy, a quickening that is translated through you into action, and because there is only one of you in all of time, this expression is unique.*
>
> *And if you block it, it will never exist through any other medium and it will be lost. The world will not have it.*
>
> *It is not your business to determine how good it is nor how valuable nor how it compares with other expressions.*
>
> *It is your business to keep it yours clearly and directly, to keep the channel open. You do not even have to believe in yourself or your work.*
>
> *You have to keep yourself open and aware to the urges that motivate you.*
>
> *Keep the channel open.*

Rebels Everywhere

Something often happens or I have an encounter and I think I should blog about it, but then it strikes me as too thin for an entire post. And so these ideas bounce off my head like poorly struck soccer balls, never to be seen or heard from again. Not this time! Rebel miscellany:

The diagnostic power of laughter

I recently attended a great workshop on creativity from Brice Challamel and his company Act One. His content contains many useful hints for Rebels at Work, but my favorite and one I have turned to again and again is the importance of paying attention to when people in a meeting laugh at an idea.

Laughter occurs when your brain hears something that disrupts its normal way of thinking, what it has anticipated would happen. Thus, the eruption of laughter tells Rebels at Work that the audience views their idea as disruptive and unusual.

If you can, call out the significance of that laughter right away. Point out that the laughter means that the audience finds the idea particularly unusual, indeed...rebellious. Ask people if they can explain why. Even if you don't feel comfortable doing that type of instant analysis of a room's reaction, take account of it as you move forward.

The idea they laughed at has tremendous power and potential. And if there is no nervous laughter in your meeting, well then maybe you aren't being rebellious enough.

Uncertainty and risk: not the same thing

This insight comes courtesy of Richard Boly, who just left government after setting up eDiplomacy at the State Department. We were catching up just before Thanksgiving and Richard reminded me that often times people oppose a new way of doing things just because it is uncertain. But they don't usually describe their concerns as being about uncertainty.

They will say instead: "Your idea is too risky."

It might be useful for Rebels at Work at that point to gently remind their interlocutor that uncertainty and risk are not the same thing. Exploring a new idea is one of the ways in which you determine whether there is indeed any risk involved. Not being willing to pursue a new idea just because it is uncertain is just about the dumbest thing really—OK...don't say that! If something is not uncertain, then it ain't new.

The Bitcoin rebels

Yesterday I spoke at the Future of Money and Technology Conference in San Francisco, which was dominated by discussions about the virtual currency Bitcoin. This is not the place to talk about the very complex new phenomenon of virtual currencies except to say that I left the conference much more intrigued about its world-changing possibilities.

But I was struck at the rebel energy in the room...and the visions. Listening to the heads of startups talk about how they could change the course of humanity with their ideas must have been what it was like listening to individuals in the early 1990s talk about what the Internet could become. If only we could bring such energy inside existing organizations. If only...

The hacker ethic

Finally, and also brought home by the Bitcoin discussions, I was struck by the similarity between Rebels at Work and the Hacker mentality. Both want to explore the art of the possible and do it because of their passion for the work, the mission, and for just trying to figure out how great things could become if we just pretended there were no boundaries and precedents. Just like Rebels at Work, you can have Good Hackers or Bad Hackers. And just like Rebels at Work, sometimes it's hard to tell the difference.

Your faithful correspondent,

Carmen

The Last Trabi: My Fearless Failure

Oh, the shortsightedness of people who espouse fearlessness. Especially when you find yourself in a fearlessness team building exercise and you keep stalling out on a major Berlin street at rush hour because you can't get the clutch of your 40-year-old, East German Trabi car into second gear.

Horns blare, BMWs cut you off, bicyclists appear out of nowhere. Fraulein, what are you doing? Get off the road.

I freeze in fear. How was it that I was driving this crapbox of a car for the past 10 minutes and now I am paralyzed, unable to move from 1st to second to third to oops, stop for a red light, don't hit the bicyclists, and back to first and oh shit we're stalled again. And, oh the crappy brakes. Will someone plow into us? Mein Gott, I've got two people in the car who are parents of young children.

A half an hour earlier 100 people from the company offsite were in a parking lot, dividing up into small teams of three, with one of the three volunteering to drive an old Trabi. To where we did not know. Oh, the fun of team building excursions.

Fearlessly volunteering for a team building exercise

Remembering how much I loved driving my first car, a red Fiat 128 with an amazing sound system and quirky stick shift, I volunteered to be the driver. How hard could it be?

Angela, Todd and I get in the car, me in driver's seat. The jovial Trabi tour guide shows me how to work the shift. "See, one, two, up and in for three, then like this for reverse." Not on the floor like my beloved Fiat, but on a 3-on-the-tree column shift. He points to a faded, peeling diagram on the dashboard that supposedly shows how to shift the gears. It is useless.

But I am fearless. I know how to drive a manual transmission car. I know how to drive in a crazy city. I learned how to drive in Boston. I am a Rebel at Work.

So what if it is dusk and rush hour in a big, foreign city. And that I need to drive in this rush hour and listen to navigational instructions on an ancient car radio full of static. And that we are the last car in a long line of Trabi cars and the exhaust from the cars is engulfing us in noxious fumes we EPA babies have never experienced. Let the fearless adventure begin!

Off we go. I've got this.

And then I don't.

Stopping for red lights, bikes passing in front of the car, being in the wrong lane. The voice on our radio commanding, "Take the next right. Stay in the middle lane." Every traffic light, shifting, braking, engaging back into first gear, then second, then stalling in traffic. One, twice, three times. Now panicking. Throughout it all my team mates are supportive, reassuring, masking their worry, offering to drive.

The white Trabi is lost

The man in the radio comes back on, "We have lost the white Trabi. Everyone, pull over at the next intersection and we will hope that the white Trabi will catch up."

My prefrontal cortex has shut down in fear and I can't even get the crapbox Communist car into first. Someone else has to drive. I pull over and Angela jumps into the back seat. I climb into the passenger seat and Todd climbs over from the backseat to the driver's seat. It would be hilarious to see this human jungle gym if we weren't all so rattled.

The gears grind but Todd gets our white Trabi moving, catching up with our crapbox caravan. We're supposed to be seeing the beautiful historic sites of Berlin as we drive around. But our team can only focus on the Trabi.

After missing a turn, we lose the caravan. Todd bravely makes a U-turn to try to find the other Trabis being driven by our teammates, those lucky ones who seem to be easily driving, following instructions and enjoying the tour. How are they learning about fear? Our car's gears groan and we stop on a side street. The Trabi tour leader finds us and pulls up in his electric car.

"Ach, zee two cylinder is only catching one cylinder," he tells us. "Do you want to take my electric car and I drive the Trabi?" Not wanting to fail the fearless exercise, we decline. The nice Trabi tour guide reaches into our car, yanks on the clutch, and then somehow the driving is a little easier.

The voice from the radio tells the others to pull over and wait. The last white Trabi is coming.

Fifteen minutes later, like an oasis in the desert, we see a beautifully lighted restaurant and a long line of Trabis in a parking lot. It's over. As we climb out of the car waiters serve us very good rose champagne. I drink two glasses, probably too fast.

I want my fear

At the end of the evening I tell the executive what I think about his "Be Fearless" mantra for developing a more risk-taking organizational culture. To his credit, he listens intently and with an open mind.

Telling people to "be fearless" and "fail fast" is superficial and lacks empathy.

Fear is one of the basic human emotions. We shouldn't deny its existence or value — in ourselves and in others. Fear provides important data. Our desire should not be about having less fear but understanding what we can learn from our fears.

Sometimes fear signals what we desire, motivating us to figure out what we need to do to get there. Fear has preceded every major accomplishment in my life – saying yes to stepping off a corporate career track, saying yes to starting companies, saying yes to marriage, saying yes to becoming a mother at 40, saying yes this past summer to doing an improvisational monologue in front of an audience. Fear propelled me forward.

Other times fear is our personal sonar system alerting us to danger, indicating what we need to learn, warning us from toxic situations, or giving us the energy to say no to commitments that sap our energy. Or that ask us to be someone we are not.

Fear gives us courage. It helps us to be fully alive and awake to the world in a way that confidence and bravery do not.

So yes, I hated that team building exercise because it made me fear FULL.

And I loved the exercise because it reminded me to ask for help, let my vulnerabilities show, and know that team mates are there to help. They *want* to help.

We're all in this together, especially when we see a Berlin city bus barreling down the street at us when we're stuck in a stalled Trabi.

On Giving a Shit

Look at what you really give a shit about and then go do something about it.

This is what I learned this year at the annual Business Innovation Factory innovation conference.

This is the best way to feel fully alive and leave the world a better place.

Nothing changes when we sit on the sidelines. Or worse, it does change, but not how we want.

- More people starve from poverty. (@eastvanbrand)
- Crazy, narcissistic, self-serving billionaires get into office. (@alanwebber)
- Teachers check out. (@100kin10)
- People with cardiac issues don't check back in with their doctors. (@MGHHeartHealth)
- Systems of inequities and injustices oppress and kill people, bodily and/or in spirit. (@taliqtillman, @carrolldesign, @tenygross)

Complacency and apathy create danger.

Accept the offer, know you are enough

Oh, but when we "accept the offer" of what life dishes out (@jazzcode), recognize that we can't go back to what was (@CajunAngela), free the talented blue lobster people (@dscofield), realize we are enough (@taliqtillman), we can move mountains. Especially when we get clear on what we fiercely care about.

The "give a shit" litmus test

When it comes to getting clear, the "give a shit" litmus test is a much better decision filter to me than the soft, passive words like purpose, passion, personal brand (gag).

Language is powerful. It can oppress, judge, bore, shake us awake and kick our ass.

A Fortune 50 client today asked me to help her articulate a clearer purpose for her organization. Emboldened by BIF2017, I asked what she and her colleagues really "give a shit about" beyond the polished brand narrative. Now we were talking, for fu*k's sake.

As an aside, if you're someone who is offended by swearwords or think it's lazy to use them, I urge you to read "Holy Shit: A Brief History of Swearing" by Melissa Mohr.

People swear about what they care about. As Carmen Medina (@milouness) said, some people deserve to be called assholes. And sometimes those assholes can open doors for you if you're looking forward. Mohr tells us that:

> *"Swearwords are the most powerful words we have with which to express extreme emotion, whether negative or positive...we need irreproachably formal and unassailably decent speech, but we also need the dirty, the vulgar, the wonderful obscenities and oaths that can do for us what no other words can."*

I give a shit about helping people be heard.

Helping people to challenge the status quo and advocate for positive change in their organizations? Well sure, that's part of it, but that doesn't mobilize anyone, including me.

In today's world we have to stop the yak, yak, yakking and do something.

No more waiting around for the proverbial "them" to save us.

Live your name as it's in the stars

In his story about courageous conversations Courtlandt Butts (@CC_AboutRace) talked about how he was ridiculed about his name in school. When he looked up the meaning of his name he learned that it is "messenger from the island."

"You will live up to your name as it's in the stars," he said.

Today I looked up mine and found it means "Better Warrior." No wonder I so love the Rebels at Work tribe.

Following Angela Blanchard's wise counsel I will continue to help people do the right thing, not the rule thing.

And I will honor grief and gratitude, forgiving the past so that we may all go dancing today.

REFRAME YOUR VALUE

Bad Rebel Doing Good

Is there a place for the "bad" rebel — the person who storms into an organization and bulldozes his or her change agenda?

Usually, no. But there are exceptions. Like the superintendent of an urban city school system.

Rather than slowly roll out his change initiatives by building relationships and developing coalitions of support, this educator introduced a dizzying number of reforms and new practices in a very short time, using what some would say was an autocratic style.

His big, bold ideas set off bureaucratic fireworks among school administrators, teachers, parents, unions and the public.

His "outsider" status didn't help, either. "He doesn't know how things work in our part of the country," many of his opponents told me.

"Why are you alienating so many people with your ideas," I asked him.

"Superintendents of large urban school systems have a tenure of about three years — at most," he said. "If I want to have any impact on improving education in this city I need to get as many important initiatives going as possible in the hope that something will stick before I'm asked to leave."

Sure enough, 18 months later there was a shift in politics and he was no longer superintendent.

Have some of his ideas stuck? Yes. As much as he would have liked? No.

Building support and sequencing our change programs is usually the best way to go. But if your position is precarious and the cause important, you may need to move fast and bold, getting as much "good" adopted before opponents discredit your intentions and fire you.

Messengers at Work

A lot of people don't like the word rebel. I like rebel because it connotes people with courage, conviction and a commitment to stand up for change.

"Messenger is a much better word," my friend Maria has been telling me for several months. "It's positive. Rebels are angry fighters."

This week Maria shared a new take on "messenger."

"Remember I suggested that you think about using of messenger instead of rebel? Well I looked up the Greek meaning of messenger. Messenger means angel. And angels' first words are: 'Be not afraid.'"

Perhaps one of the greatest responsibilities we have in bringing new ideas to our organizations is helping our colleagues and bosses not to be afraid, and to:

- Show the path to a new and better way with kindness and purposefulness.
- Help people understand the difference between risk and uncertainty.
- Balance experimenting and acting recklessly.
- Acknowledge the sadness of letting go of what we once excelled at because it's no longer relevant.
- Recognize fear and lead fearlessly despite uncertainty.

As messengers of change our responsibility — like angels — is influencing, guiding and making it safe for people to step into new ways.

You Say Rebel, I Say Scout!

Our most recent blog post, Only Good Rebels Die Young, set off a great, private conversation on Google+ over the past week. The ideas and reflections were awesome and I would like to share a couple here.

Rebels have to play both a short game and a long game

People differed as to what each "game" consisted of, but generally I think the concept that rebels have to do one set of things in the short term and another set of things for the long-term is spot on.

But what does the long term look like in organizations? Is the long term fulfilling the essential mission of the company or is the long term the race to control the company by its senior leaders? If it's the latter, and it's my guess that either could be in play depending upon the organization, then the rebel has to deal with one set of issues, such as risk aversion and the desire to avoid accountability.

If over the long term the actual fulfillment of mission is most important, then the rebel's suggestions will be judged, often harshly, against the imperative to "get the job done."

Are we scouts or pathfinders, and not rebels?

Some of my friends, and I'm sure many others, aren't really comfortable with the rebel label. They don't necessarily see themselves in opposition with the organization; they just want to make it better.

Perhaps, one noted, Rebels at Work are just people who have the ability to see things differently than the majority in the workplace. There is actually one clear minority in the workplace, according to Myers Briggs tests. These are the intuitive people in general and the introverted intuitives in particular.

Unlike most of the other Myers Briggs attributes, which are distributed more or less evenly in the general population, about 75% of Americans test as sensers and only 25% test as intuitive. (The same breakdown occurs for extroversion/introversion.) I thought that was pretty interesting and so I pursued it further. And almost immediately I ran across this paper: Introverted Intuitives: Managing Diversity in the Workplace. This paper contains boatloads of insight for corporate rebels, scouts, pathfinders, even more perhaps than the literature on Gifted Children and Adults I discovered a couple of weeks ago.

As the author Laurie Nadel notes, introverted intuitives in the workplace have a strong sense of their individualism, strong creative problem-solving abilities, and a desire for autonomy.

All intuitives—introverted or extroverted—because of their willingness to rely on what their gut tells them — have the ability, as one of my friends put it in the Google+ discussions, "to find or make a new path for themselves and their organizations that others cannot see."

Nadel suggests that the extroverted intuitive is more likely to be successful in an organizational setting than the introverted intuitive. Although both groups are rare, the introverted intuitives are the most rare, making up only 4% of the population. (That's the number Nadel cites in her monographs. My casual reading suggest they make up a somewhat bigger proportion, but they are still mighty small.) Disclosure: I am a borderline ENFP/INFP although I think what extroversion I do have is a learned behavior.

But to return to my friend's main point, maybe we're not rebels at all, we're scouts. The Kit Carsons of the Corporate World. We can see around the corner and sometimes even over the horizon.

As I've written previously, I don't really think anyone starts out with the intent to be a Rebel at Work, except perhaps those who have a problem with any concept of authority. Most of us don't even know we're scouts. Until we find out differently, we assume everyone sees what we see.

But it's the organization's reaction to our ideas, and our commitment to continue trying to advance them in spite of that reaction, that in the end turns us into rebels. I suppose some scouts never become rebels. Those are probably the extroverted ones!!

It would be great to empirically determine if most self-identified corporate rebels are in fact intuitive. If you don't know, there are many free Myers Briggs tests online that are generally accurate. I won't recommend any one in particular but you can just Google the term. If you feel like sharing your results in the comments section, we'd love to hear from you.

Game of Thrones Reminder: You've Got the Power

Watching *Games of Thrones* Sunday I was reminded that we Rebels often have the power we need to act. We don't have to "get permission" from bosses or the hierarchy within which we work.

Now, back to Winterfell, that cold, dark castle in the north. The old gang was sitting around the fire and sharing war stories over wine when Tormund Giantsbane was shocked to learn that Brienne of Tarth wasn't a "ser" like her male peers. He boasted that he'd make her a knight if he was a king.

Jaime Lannister chimed in to point out that it doesn't take a king to make someone a knight.

A knight can make someone a knight.

And then Jaime knighted Brienne. Knight to Knight.

Do we mistakenly tell ourselves we can't do things that are within our power?

As importantly, are we helping and supporting our peers to claim their power? To act like the Knights they are even though the Kings and Queens have not bestowed fancy titles?

"In the name of the Warrior, I charge you to be brave."

Am I a Minority or Am I a Rebel? Both!

As most of you know, I served for 32 years at the Central Intelligence Agency. During my last ten years there, I would attend recruiting and outreach events where I would answer questions about my career at the Agency. Given who I am, I was often asked this question: "Could you talk about what it was like being a woman and a minority at the Agency?"

And I always gave the same answer: "Actually, neither of those was as much of an issue for me as just being a different thinker. Somehow I often saw things differently from everyone else."

I was recalling this last week when I was thinking about what I might say at a couple of events I've been invited to speak at associated with Hispanic Heritage Month, which starts this coming week. (It's actually not a month, but a 30-day period from 15 September to 15 October.) And as I said out loud the previous paragraph, it came to me like the most gigantic "DUH" moment you can imagine. POW! A giant fist bopped me on the head.

I had gotten it exactly backwards. It wasn't that being a different thinker was more of a career issue than being a woman or a minority. I was a different thinker in large part BECAUSE I was a woman and a Latina.

Q. You mean that it took you until one month before your 58th Birthday to figure that out!!

A. Sadly, yes.

Many sincere attempts to diversify organizations fail because the organization's leadership does not appreciate that any significant diversity effort is in fact an organizational change effort. It could very well end up being transformational for the company.

When different types of people enter the workforce—women, minorities—many actually become default Rebels at Work, although they often are not aware of their dual identities.

People with different backgrounds should bring different perspectives and ideas with them. (Although truth be told, many learn as early as high school to stop volunteering their different ideas when they realize they are not welcomed.) And yet you often hear leaders say: "It's a shame about so-and-so. Some interesting ideas but he doesn't quite know how to fit in." Or, "You have great potential but you need to learn to be more corporate."

And that's how diversity initiatives degrade and become more about the Appearance of Diversity than about the Impact of Diversity. The organization has made space for people who are different but no space for their different ideas.

Helping Rebels be more effective at work is in fact a diversity initiative. And increasing the Impact of Diversity on an organization is in fact a Rebel initiative.

Working Ahead

Just a quick post from Cannon Beach in Oregon to point out an article I read about Gifted Adults that I think resonates with many of the issues affecting rebels. I came across the article when I was reflecting on how I became a rebel.

One of the conclusions I drew was that once I became an adult and reached the work environment, the qualities that had served me so well during university were actually not so popular in the work environment. For example, being inquisitive was highly useful in college but not so useful when I started work, particularly if the "thing" I was being inquisitive about was the logic behind certain work practices.

Wondering if this experience was common, I started searching for information on "loners at work" or "intelligent people at work" which is how I came across this interesting article about Counseling Gifted Adults by Paula Prober. I bet most of us resist the label of "gifted" but several sentences resonated so strongly with many of the experiences rebels have already documented. For example:

We associate giftedness in adults with high levels of achievement. But it is not that simple. In fact, *the gifted person is as likely to be the high school rebel* as she is the valedictorian, the CEO, or the Nobel prize winner.

Does that sound familiar? Or the description of typical traits of gifted adults:

Complex analytical mind, rapid speech, advanced empathy, quirky sense of humor, and perfectionism.

Do these remarks resemble you?

But what really sold it for me was when I read the description provided by the gifted adult Susan of her early educational adventures:

Susan said she recalled being thrilled about starting school but very quickly feeling deeply disappointed. In second grade, for example, she completed an entire reading workbook in one night. With enthusiasm, she showed her teacher the next day and was reprimanded for working ahead.

The phrase **"Working Ahead"** hit me like one of Proust's Madeleines. I hadn't heard that phrase in almost 50 years, probably, but I suddenly remembered it as one of the constant refrains of my childhood.

Don't work ahead. Don't read ahead.

And so, of course, that's what many corporate rebels do. They ***work ahead.*** They can't help it, or at least they can't control it until they become painfully aware of its impact at the workplace and on their own careers.

The article cites as a principal reference the book The Gifted Adult by Mary-Elaine Jacobsen which I will order and scour for other relevant content.

In the meantime: **Keep working ahead.**

BE READY TO PLAY THE LONG GAME

Change Myths and Privileges

We hear a lot of stories here at Rebels at Work.

Many people are angry at not being heard. Some are sad that their organizations are on a bad downward spiral, with management rallying around what no longer works. Others have checked out of work and checked into being complacent and "just getting the paycheck."

For a while the complacent ones got to me the most. To go to work every day and not give a rat's ass just seems like giving up on life itself.

And the cynicism? Scorching. It would be tough to work with someone with that kind of negative mindset.

But the stories that get to me the most are the people who don't try to change anything because of the **CHANGE MYTH.** These people believe that if you're going to try to fix problems you need to be some sort of crusading take-no-prisoners, storm the ramparts hero.

You might imagine the type: a confident Steve Jobs wannabe talking about disruption, not backing down, go big or go home. The kind of person who doesn't worry about failing, whether that means getting fired or quitting to find the next gig.

How did this change maker myth become so ingrained in our culture?

Has the Silicon Valley "failure is good" entrepreneurial spirit been taken as "the" way things work at work? Are people with good ideas becoming intimidated about stepping up because they are not Steve Jobs wannabes and they are afraid to fail and lose their jobs?

Last week Jen Meyers sent these two tweets that acknowledged the myth and, more importantly, acknowledged the fact that most people making change are doing so thoughtfully within the rules and corporate culture.

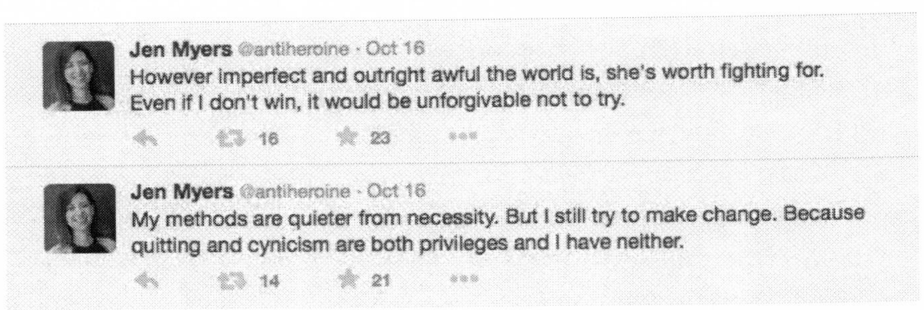

Jen Myers @antiheroine · Oct 16
However imperfect and outright awful the world is, she's worth fighting for. Even if I don't win, it would be unforgivable not to try.
16
23
Jen Myers @antiheroine · Oct 16
My methods are quieter from necessity. But I still try to make change. Because quitting and cynicism are both privileges and I have neither.
14
21

Because that's how so much change happens. Bit by bit. Working with our co-workers vs. leaping from tall buildings in superhero change-maker capes.

If you're a disruptor and get fired, your big idea dies. So much for heroism.

Whereas if you get smarter about working within the existing organizational culture, your idea actually has a better chance of happening. And you have a better chance of keeping your job.

(Because if we're honest like Jen, we know that most of us can't afford to walk away from our jobs. It's not that simple.)

So maybe it's useful to remember that having a good idea is easy. Being able to work with people willing to do the hard work to shepherd that idea through corporate politics, budget conflicts, and the often messy rollout is a privilege.

The Rebel Gardener

I didn't come easily to gardening. In fact, until I was about 55 years old that I paid gardening no mind at all. Zilch.

All I could see in gardening was way too much physical labor, almost all of it during hot Washington D.C. summers. Just a lot of sweat.

But somewhere in my body lurked the gardening gene just waiting to express itself. Geneticists have determined that for some genes, expression is indeed a function of age. And clearly that was the case for my gardening gene. In the spring of 2010, it began to stick out its tendril-covered head. I began modestly with a few tomato plants. But in just a couple of years, I was starting most of my plants as seedlings and slowly reclaiming the ivy-infested parts of my lawn. It's an ongoing project.

I wish someone had told me sooner that gardening was a learning activity. Only by paying attention to how the plants behave under different conditions can you improve your gardening success rate. If you get into it, gardening is a deeply analytic activity.

And, of course or I wouldn't be writing about it here, gardening offers a series of lessons for Rebels at Work.

Being a Rebel at Work calls upon your analytic talents. And the more experience you have as a Rebel, the smarter you will be about advocating for change in organizations. But beyond that...

Failure is an essential component of gardening and of being a Rebel at Work

It's only been in the past year that, as a gardener, I've become comfortable in ripping out plants that didn't work out where I put them. I used to think such bad outcomes were an indictment of my underdeveloped gardening skills. Now I understand that only through experimentation can I learn what works and what doesn't.

Now Rebels at Work probably can't afford too many bad ideas, but if you can master the art of tiny pivots—small experiments that can test some aspect of a proposal, you can learn to leverage "failure." Before gardeners invest real money in a new flower bed, they should first test just a plant here or there to see what works in the soil and light.

The shady spots are never as shady as you think and the sunny spots are never as sunny

This partly explains why failure is an essential component of gardening. Just a few feet of separation can produce significant changes in light. I once planted two rose bushes within three feet of each other on the southeast exposure of my lawn. One prospered but the other faltered because of the dappled sunlight that reached it through overhanging trees. When I moved the laggard to what I had previously thought of as the too-shady side of my lawn, it doubled in size.

Rebels can sometimes make facile assumptions about what parts of the organization would be most receptive to change. The team you think is ideal for your prototype because the leader is so friendly may actually harbor bamboo spikes underneath its surface. Go beyond superficial appearances.

Some things just take time

Plants have to settle into their new environments. Weather varies year to year. My transplanted rose bush only gave one weak flower the first year in its new location. But now it's a reliable producer, if still not as robust as its sun-blessed twin.

And so it is with organizational change. Expecting immediate results should be a rookie mistake, and yet we see it everywhere. I often think the most successful change efforts are the ones that people don't quite realize are happening. Tiny pivots accumulate and without *sturm und drang* the organization finds itself in a better place. Rebels who want instant ego gratification normally aren't willing to take the tortoise approach, so their garden doesn't grow.

Do the work

I'm downright lazy about routine tasks. But gardening has knocked some sense into me on this front. Unless I do the work, nothing good happens.

Failing to do the work is lethal to gardeners and Rebels. The Rebel who talks about her vision without creating a viable implementation plan is failing to do the work. If you're not into details, ally yourself with someone who is!

Tight Pants

By last Friday afternoon I was exhausted, having worked on an especially rebel-worthy assignment.

This meant I had to maneuver around Bureaucratic Black Belts (BBBs) and move people off assumptions that they wanted to fight (me) for. All very congenial, but intense nevertheless.

It also meant that I had to find ways to help people see a better way, be confident while also being honest about the uncertainties, and remain steadfast and open-minded.

Talk about paradox. Can I also say once again how exhausted I was?

Two themes I find about change: there can be no progress without paradox, and leading change is exhausting.

On Friday afternoon a good friend was kind enough to listen to me talk about what had happened, and ask good questions to help me clarify the best next steps.

She also said, "You know, being a rebel is a lot like what Terry Pearce said in his book *Leading Out Loud*."

> *"There are many people who think they want to be matadors, only to find themselves in the ring with two thousand pounds of bull bearing down on them, and then discover that what they really wanted was to wear tight pants and hear the crowd roar."*

Real rebels are not afraid stay in the ring.

II

Practices & Habits

Section Highlights: Practices and Habits

The Rebels at Work movement has always been about helping people with good ideas — the change agents, the engaged employee. In fact, the Rebel at Work is arguably the most engaged employee any agency or company can have. But even the person with fantastic ideas can stumble if they don't know how best to proceed.

So, for the last ten years, many of our blog posts have offered practical suggestions for gaining allies, moving forward, and avoiding mistakes.

Many of these, of course, made it into our first book—for example the importance of befriending bureaucratic black belts; this continues to resonate with our audiences across the USA and indeed across the world. We even occasionally get some people who raise their hands and admit to being BBB's, ready to help the change agents in the room.

But we've learned even more in the last few years from talking to the many Rebels we've met and by interacting with organizations, large and small, who know their bottom lines could benefit from more Rebel energy.

Smart first steps for Rebels is an area we've explored deeply. I (Carmen) have written on how important it is for Rebels to assess whether their change ideas are theological in nature: in other words, whether they run exactly counter to your organization's prevailing orthodoxy.

In my case, I argued during the 1990s that all knowledge organizations—including the CIA—would have to fundamentally change in response to the revolutionary nature of the Internet and digital technologies.

What I did not fully appreciate at the time was that CIA values were against everything the Internet stood for: the CIA was for secrecy, the Internet was for openness; the CIA wanted to protect information, the internet to share it. Things would have been less painful if I had appreciated earlier the difficulty of advancing such heretical notions.

Aspiring change agents must identify early on whether they are pursuing theological change. We're not arguing that Rebels should never do so because sometimes an issue is just that important. But Rebels need to go into such efforts with their eyes wide open. It will be hard, your career may suffer, and it will be even more important for you to find allies to help you move forward.

In this chapter you'll also encounter:

- Additional advice for those getting started, such as how to break the soil for rebel ideas, the importance of knowing what matters to your boss, and questions you can use to help colleagues appreciate the need for change.
- Reminders of the importance of building an alliance of fellow rebels who can work together to make change happen.
- Examples of the heavy lifting Rebels often have to do.
- Encouragement for Rebels to be patient and gritty in steering their projects to success. Sometimes you have to settle for less than you actually want; I fondly remember a Rebel educator who came up to her after a talk and said just two words: "Tiny Pivots!"
- And a couple of pieces devoted to the particular circumstances of Rebels in government.

GETTING STARTED

So Now What Do I Do?

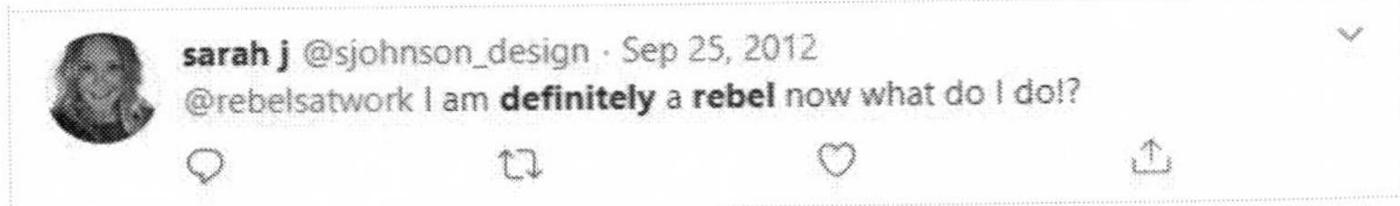

sarah j @sjohnson_design · Sep 25, 2012
@rebelsatwork I am definitely a rebel now what do I do!?

What an inviting question Sarah asks.

It's one thing to realize that you are a rebel — risk taking, curious, creative, unafraid to challenge assumptions. It's another thing to use those rebel qualities to make a difference at work.

So what do you do?

It's such a big, important question with so many possibilities. Some ideas to consider:

Create an informal rebel alliance, where people in the organization get together once a month after work to talk about positive ways to change the organization. Occasionally invite an open-minded creative exec to join you in thinking about new ways.

Become the organization's informal trendspotter, sharing monthly insights on emerging industry or professional trends and their potential implications for your organization. Rebels tend to see emerging patterns ahead of most, in fact we're often criticized for working too far ahead of other people. Use this talent to help others tune in faster to changes.

Learn how to host and facilitate meetings in new ways that allow for healthy dissent, frank conversations, and space for thinking out loud together. (I'm an especially big fan of the Art of Hosting.) Teach others in your organization how to host vs. run meetings, have the real conversations vs. the polite conversations. This one change can affect the culture in a big way, making it more "rebel, diverse idea friendly."

Develop an experiment budget: Suggest that the organization set aside a small budget for experiments in areas that could potentially provide big benefits for the organization. Invite people/teams to submit ideas to be considered for funded experiments. Think about crowdsourcing.

Position your new idea as experiment: Or position an idea you want to make happen as an experiment. This diffuses some of the fear and uncertainty that often prevents executives from approving new ideas. Couched as an experiment, a new idea often seems much less threatening.

Support another rebel: It's often lonely and frustrating being the rebel who is trying to create change. Consider supporting someone with a great idea who could benefit from your ideas, your encouragement, your help or simply your public acknowledgement that what they're doing is worthwhile.

Stay edgy: go to conferences, read books, follow people whose ideas fascinate you. Learn one scary thing a year. Rebels tend to be pattern makers, bringing ideas from different disciplines together in new ways to solve problems. If you don't get out enough, e.g., are totally sucked up by just your business your industry, you may lose your rebel power to see those patterns and unusual combinations.

Be a trusted sounding board: be the person who is willing to listen to people who are frustrated or are wrestling with a new idea or are just trying to figure out what's not working and what the possibilities might be. When people can think out loud with someone they trust, ideas often start to emerge. You don't need to fix or solve their conundrums, just ask open, honest questions that helps them think about the situation in new ways. And then listen. This is such a generous and helpful act, and so many important "ahas" emerge. A rebel executive friend and I have dinner once a month to help one another in this way. 30 minutes for her, 30 minutes for me. Some kind of wow emerges. Then we finish dinner and talk about politics, movies, and books.

Stop doing things that you believe are ineffective or unhelpful for the organization. Don't go to meetings about issues that are not relevant, or where you can't get or provide value. Don't use PowerPoint, have a conversation. Instead of the usual performance evaluation approach, create and use your professional manifesto to set goals and frame context for what you want to do and why it matters. Stop responding late night to urgent emails about non-urgent issues; take back your time. Don't write a 30 slide PowerPoint deck when a one-page summary with bullet points would be an easier, faster way for people to understand the issue.

Keep people informed: be the person who updates people about an issue important to you and them, and suggest what actions they can take.

Stop waiting for permission: Change happens when a few people get together and start doing the small things that lead to positive outcomes. Often quietly, under the radar. If you wait for approval or management to "model change," you're likely to never see anything happen.

What other advice would you give to Sarah?

Breaking the Soil

The book on my nightstand right now is Willa Cather's *My Antonia*. I've come to Willa Cather way too late in life. Cather writes compelling novels, mostly about pioneers, that brim with insights about people doing hard things. In *My Antonia*, she describes the tribulations of the settlers of the vast Midwest prairies, focusing on an immigrant family from Bohemia and their daughter, Antonia.

I had occasion to mention the book recently when I was chatting with someone who has so far been unable to change the conversation in his organization. He described a group of people so set in their ways that their skin had the bluish tint of rigor mortis. Agendas of meetings are so tightly controlled that it's impossible to introduce new ideas. What could he do?

"Break the soil," I said, channeling my inner Willa Cather.

In *My Antonia*, Cather describes the difficult process by which the farmers prepared their soil after the frigid winter. Before any seeds could be planted, the settlers trudged behind their oxen or horses to break and turn the cold soil. Unless this work was done, sowing seeds was pointless. Seeds don't grow in ill-prepared soil.

And that's what needs to be done in frozen organizations where change seems impossible. Unless the Rebel at Work steps back to "break the soil," his seed ideas are unlikely to take root.

What breaking the soil looks like

So what does breaking the soil look like in organizations and businesses? We'd love to hear your ideas but here are some ideas.

Take advantage of any extracurricular activities, such as a "giving back to the community" days or the annual office picnic, to improve your relations with others, understand what makes them feel good, and perhaps gently encourage some reflection on how things are going.

Share articles, videos, etc. that promote interesting ideas. Don't pick negative articles; don't editorialize! Just share! And try to find ideas that the organization can claim it is already implementing—whether it's true or not! The group's perception of itself is key. If people start thinking of themselves as modernizers, they're more likely to consider other "new" ideas.

Engage in reciprocity. Do favors for others. Help someone advance an idea you're not that fond of in hopes they will do the same for you some day.

And one of our favorite evergreen ideas: have lunch with a bureaucratic black belt in your organization. Ask them about what's most important to the group and why. Have them talk about previous successful initiatives and what has worked in the past.

When planting your new seeds, it's best to start with those that will thrive in the current soil.

Nothing Gets Approved Without This: Know What Your Boss Wants

There's a bad habit pervasive at work: not knowing what's important to your boss and/or other people involved in approving your projects.

You keep sending project updates, adding more data to your PowerPoint presentations, researching additional industry best practices, writing emails warning that you need approvals now so as not to incur greater costs or fall behind deadlines.

And you hear nothing from your boss or client.

You complain to your team mates and become more and more frustrated. It's like spitting in the wind.

I've heard this story over and over again in advising project teams and self-identified Rebels at Work.

"Do you know what's most important to your boss? Is your project or proposal addressing what's most important to her," I ask.

SILENCE.

And then a quick, "Wait, what?" and recognition of something so obvious people can't believe they have forgotten to do it.

They don't know what's most important to their boss. (As an aside: there's often a disconnect between stated goals and what's most important.)

This is why so many good ideas and projects get stalled. Bosses focus on what's most important to them and ignore ideas that they don't see as relevant.

Some suggestions:

1. Ask your boss (or clients or others with whom you need cooperation) what's most important to them and why.
2. Show people how your idea supports what's important.
3. When seeking feedback, ask how important on a scale of 1-10 the proposed idea is to them. If it's six or below, realize you're probably not going to make much progress. It's not a priority. Put your energy somewhere else.
4. Ask what would move the idea from a six to an eight or nine.
5. During a meeting when people start talking why an idea won't work stop the negativity quickly by asking, "How important on a scale of 1-10 is this idea to us?" If it's not important, move on to a different topic. If it IS important, reframe the conversation to "this idea will work IF we..." vs. "this won't work because..."

Lastly, remember that bosses love learning what the organization can STOP doing. When you have a clear understanding of what's important, earn credibility and trust by recommending what to stop.

It's disappointing to learn that a great idea or new approach isn't important. But the sooner you know, the sooner you can focus on what does matter.

P.S. *For all you bosses out there, be proactive and explain what is most important on a regular basis. You have no idea how much work and wasted energy goes on by bright people on your team.*

It's the Problem

"The secret is to find the important problems and focus on those," explained Monique Savoie, founding president of the Society for Arts & Technology (SAT) in Montreal, which some call the MIT of Canada (although it is so much more), and a visionary on the interdisciplinary challenges of bridging science, art and technology.

Monique was responding to a Fortune 100 executive's question about how to better prioritize resources and talent, cultivate more creative, flexible organizational cultures, and attract and keep talent.

While the response may seem simplistic, it is not. Great solutions result from getting the problem right, and then focusing work on solving that problem.

We then act like scientists: challenging assumptions and developing and researching hypotheses with the people who might benefit from a new approach.

Solving the right problems, the most important problems, also motivates team members. It is "employee engagement" at its best. Almost all of us want to be working on something that matters.

"What is the most important problem for us to take on?" may be one of the most helpful questions to consider in this annual planning season.

Who needs the water and how can we get it to them?

Another wise leader, Meg Wheatley, also urges us to more clearly see what needs to be done and then go do it.

Are You an Optimist or a Pessimist?

Some people want to put us into a category.

Some people only feel good when they know where they fit.

Are you an optimist?

A pessimist?

Really, there's only one right answer. You have to be an optimist.

Otherwise you're a drag. No fun to be around. Dr. Death.

And a new term, you're from the "Doomsphere."

In the past, we were taught to note our worldview by looking at a glass of water.

Is the glass half empty? Is it half full?

Your answer defines your identity: Gloom and doom or hopeful and great to hang

out with.

What a nonsensical question this is. Is the glass half full or half empty?

Who cares?!

The right question for Warriors is:

Who needs the water and how can we get it to them?

What is the work that needs doing and how can I contribute to making it

happen?

No labels. Just seeing clearly what needs to be done and stepping up to do it.

Margaret Wheatley ©2019

Your Strategy is Due for a Checkup

A person responsible for training innovators asked me recently how he could encourage senior leaders in his government organization to think like Rebels at Work. And I said: You probably can't!

I just don't know too many leaders in government who are are ready to embrace their inner heretic. And approaching them directly about the need to think rebelliously is likely to lead to defensiveness.

So I suggested a different tack. Ask them:

> *How do you know when your tactics and strategy need refreshing?*

I've yet to meet anyone who has a ready answer to that question. Or this one...

> *What's your process for determining when your strategic plan needs to change?*

When people think about it, sometimes they volunteer that their strategic plans are refreshed at the start of their fiscal years and/or when a new senior leadership team takes over.

Now isn't that the darndest thing? Why should thinking about how things might need to be done differently be a function of the calendar? Conditions can change at a moment's notice and at any time of the year. The necessary adjustments your team needs to make might not wait twelve months...or perhaps not even thirty days.

We all know that organizations that adjust more quickly to changing circumstances have a competitive advantage, and yet most don't have a method for doing so.

And that's where Rebels at Work step in. If employees on your team are encouraged to speak up when they see trouble looming or a new opportunity coming, your organization is likely to be more nimble and more successful. Along with that agility comes an added benefit: the annual strategic refresh need not be as discombobulating. Or perhaps need not occur at all.

So let's add this to the list of good questions to ask in organizations.

How do we know when our strategy needs refreshing?

The Better We Need is Usually Staring Us in the Face

I ran across this story the other day about how the city of Utrecht in the Netherlands has installed bee-friendly gardens ON TOP OF ALL OF ITS BUS STOPS. What a scathingly brilliant idea!! (quoting Hayley Mills from the movie The Trouble with Angels.)

I also wondered whether the bees ever became a nuisance for the bus passengers. This concern didn't last long because my attitude toward bees has changed in the last couple of years. Whereas once I feared and avoided them, these days I'm cheering them on, looking to see if they're healthy and wondering if there is any way I could help them.

I suspect there are countless other simple but good ideas lurking in front of each of us begging to be spotted and implemented by curious humans wanting to be helpful. They are an overlooked category in the "transformation industry."

Good and simple ideas:

- Are relatively easy to implement, effort and cost-wise.
- Are not controversial; unlikely to engender strong opposition.
- Represent just a small step forward, but...
- Can have powerful secondary effects.
- Are not always low-hanging fruit because their potential is often not immediately appreciated.

And yet often we find CHANGE AGENTS not even considering such small ideas, focusing instead on a honking big transformation effort. You know the kind with the big fancy titles such as OPERATION ATHENA or TALENT! AWAKEN or THE 22ND CENTURY PROTOCOL. (I just made those up so if there are actually some ongoing projects bearing those names then you have my sympathy!)

I've come to believe that grandiose transformation efforts are almost always ill-conceived and advised.

When I was at CIA in the early aughts I was in charge of a transformation effort—content management systems were all the rage. My bosses kept wanting me to give it some kind of fancy name but I kept resisting, intuiting that the only thing a fancy name would do is make it easier for people to remember the project if it failed. You can say I was not brimming with confidence.

Particularly when you're starting out on your journey as a Rebel at Work, a good and simple idea may be the best place to start.

- Maybe you could organize an informal book club within your team.
- Or commit yourself to providing colleagues with positive feedback at least once a week.
- Or you could create a "task rabbit" type bulletin board in your workplace where colleagues can list tasks they need help with and volunteer to pitch in on those they can help on.

Or maybe you can plant a bee-friendly garden.

BUILD REBEL ALLIANCES

Create Your Rebel Alliance

"Change happens one lunch table at a time," Carmen has often said referring to her informal Rebel Alliance at the CIA.

The point is that to move new ideas forward we need help from others. We can't do it alone. The best "experts" on how to make change and move new ideas forward in our organizations are almost always the people in our organizations.

The people inside know how the organization really works. The hidden gatekeepers who can help us or stop us. The risks and trends the execs are secretly obsessing about. How to streamline contracts through Purchasing and Legal. What helps IT to respond more quickly.

Like-minded Rebels can help us figure out how to get things done within the quirkiness of our particular organization, how to make our ideas better, and when to hit the pause or go faster button.

As importantly, our Rebel friends can offer support, empathy, and, if we're lucky, sick humor to keep everything in perspective.

Tips for starting online Rebel community

Some of us we can have regular lunch or after-work get togethers. There is nothing better than being together in person. But for those spread across geographic locations, an online Rebel community might be helpful.

We asked Rachel Happe, co-founder and chief wonk of The Community Roundtable, for suggestions on how to create a stealth Rebel Alliance. (P.S. No one knows more about communities and networked communications than Rachel. An added bonus is that she is a good Rebel.)

Here's what she suggests.

Purpose: start by establishing the purpose and value of the Rebel Alliance. What do you want to do together and why?

When Elwin Loomis started a secret invite-only Rebel Alliance at Target the purpose was to get help and provide help to people who want to get sh*t done. Members were invited based on their track record of taking action to get things done and done fast, and their knowledge of the rules at Target and their experience circumventing the rules to get things done for the betterment of the company and team.

In starting the Rebel Alliance, Elwin explained its value this way:

> *"Large companies are hierarchies. But while the people at the top of the hierarchy tree seem to be the most important, they often are not the ones who are the most influential (or most impactful) to get stuff done. More often, it is the guy off in the corner of the org chart who has the access to the systems that you need, or the assistant to the president who can get you that info that you need. The Rebel Alliance members are the company's "do-ers. Let's care and feed people who are makers, who can create, and who 'do'. Continue to 'get sh*t done'!"*

Basics: figure out who will loosely manage the community, who to invite and what validating questions to ask people who want to join, what platform to use, and who's in charge if someone misbehaves.

Start small and simple: Rachel suggests starting really small and uncomplicated. Maybe the Rebel Alliance starts with just five people, an an inexpensive Facebook private or secret group.

Get to know one another: This is hugely important for any group, especially one where you need to trust one another and be able to talk candidly.

Have a simple but interesting format for rich profiles: some serious information, some quirky. For example: what you do in the organization, your superpower, three things people can ask you about, and or whether you're a cat or dog person. (See the bios on The Community Roundtable site as examples.)

Adding photos is hugely helpful in getting to know one another. Beyond a personal photo, consider asking people to share a photo of their desk, or of their favorite Rebel in history.

Weekly share: to orchestrate serendipity get into some simple weekly habits, like posting the three big things you'll each be working on this week. This helps people get to know who knows what, which helps you know who to turn to for specific help. Consider, too, what regular prompts might be helpful in encouraging people to share about what they know and what they're experiencing.

For more in-depth ideas about creating and running a Rebel Alliance, check out the many resources at The Community Roundtable.

Rebel on, dear friends.

Avoiding Backlash

The fear of backlash silences so many people with great ideas.

While talking about Rebels at Work yesterday a regional manager of an automotive parts company told me, "Lois I have plenty of good ideas on how to improve things at work and I know how to position ideas and connect them to what the company cares about.

"But if I if I say anything the backlash will be horrible. People's careers are ruined for speaking up at my company. I just can't risk my reputation."

So here's the deal. Don't go it alone.

Find some allies who also believe there's a way to solve the problem and together take it to your boss. If there's a handful of people supporting a new approach the boss is much more likely to consider the idea than if it's just you, and there's less likelihood of personal backlash.

Unfortunately it's easy for a boss to discredit one person who disagrees with the way the organization is being run. "He's over his head. He doesn't have enough experience. He's such a damn know-it-all. Etc. Etc. But to discredit five or 10 people? Now the boss is paying attention.

If you really want to avoid backlash, get 10 percent of the people in your organization behind the idea. Scientists at Rensselaer Polytechnic Institute have found that when 10 percent of a population holds a strong belief, the belief will be adopted.

When you have to play corporate politics, play with a team.

First Followers

"Wow, that would be amazing for us to do. It could really change how we work together," concurred a group of managers at one of the biggest technology companies in the world last week.

"But it's just not how our culture works," someone said.

Then the grumbling about the culture began until, as the strategy facilitator, I cut the naysaying short and asked, "Why couldn't this group start working differently and then open the way for others to follow? Change has to start somewhere. Why not you? You view yourselves as creative and innovative."

Someone has to start, having the guts to stand alone. And someone has to be the first to follow, also an act of leadership.

Both are things that Rebels do.

That's how culture changes and movements start.

Dare to start or be the first follower.

Inklings: a Rebel Alliance at Oxford

Forming a rebel alliance within your organization is one way to find the support to accomplish important work. Work that is outside the cultural norm of the overall organization. Or, that challenges the assumptions of the larger organization.

One example of a rebel alliance is The Inklings, a group of Oxford University professors and writers who felt stifled by the academic seriousness and solemnity of that revered institution. Feeling a bit alienated from the English Dept in 1926, Professors C.S. Lewis, J.R. R. Tolkien and other friends started meeting at a local pub.

Their intent, in Tolkien's words was to explore "vague or half formed intimations on ideas." *(Note: many rebel ideas begin in an unformed way. But a feeling exists that there must be a different or better way. Explore that feeling.)*

In other words, these Oxford rebels wanted to experiment with new ideas that didn't fit with what Oxford viewed as proper literature. Rather than feeling rejected, they came together to share ideas, experiment, get support from one another, and ultimately to create some of their best work. For Lewis it was "The Chronicles of Narnia." For Tolkien it was "The Hobbit" and "The Lord of the Rings."

They didn't try to change Oxford. Rather, they found a way to do create fascinating new work while still teaching at Oxford.

This same approach can work today in large organizations. The secret is finding people who have similar interests, making time to talk about observations and what if's, and supporting one another in a safe and enjoyable way.

Amazing things can happen when people who care about possibilities and one another find time to just hang out.

"Aim at heaven and you will get earth thrown in. Aim at earth and you get neither."
C. S. Lewis

"Courage is found in unlikely places."
J. R. R. Tolkien

Dream Teams: Diversity Isn't Enough

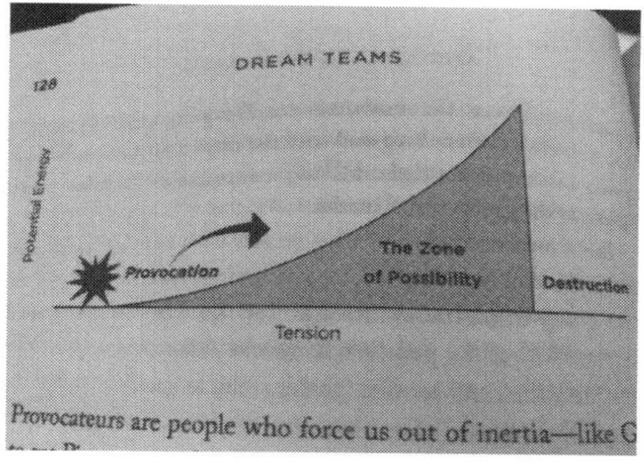

Teams with diverse viewpoints, approaches to problem solving and life experiences outperform groups of the "best and brightest," as researchers like University of Michigan's Scott Page have long shown.

BUT diversity isn't enough if people hold back from speaking up and offering their ideas.

Consider the studies by David Maxwell that found 90% of nurses unwilling to speak up to physicians even though they knew a patient might be at risk. Or the 93% of people who said they don't speak up when they know there's a risk of an accident of work.

How could they not speak up? Being different is uncomfortable and when we're uncomfortable we tend to hold back. Especially in cultures that allow abrasive behavior and abusive bosses (and physicians). It's not safe to dissent, so people don't.

Diversity also increases conflict, which people abhor. Every time Carmen and I speak and ask people about their greatest challenges when introducing new ideas, conflict tops the list.

"If organizations embrace diversity, they risk workplace conflict," says Dr. Nigel Bassett-Jones of Oxford-Brookes University. "And if they avoid diversity, they risk loss of competitiveness."

Add to that the research from Harvard, Berkeley and University of Minnesota that found most corporate diversity programs have "no positive effects in the average workplace" because when employees become scared that they might offend someone, they disengage, which contributes to more organizational silence.

The reality is that our brains are hardwired to want to be with people like ourselves— and naturally fear strangers or the unfamiliar. (Google "xenophobia" and "amygdala.") That's why so many of us naturally gravitate to groups, neighborhoods, and work teams with people like ourselves – and avoid the different.

So how DO you create Dream Teams?

So how do you create Dream Teams where different people come together, overcome the tension of their differences, and work in open, direct ways that keep you in the magical "Zone of Possibility?"

That's what Shane Snow explores in his excellent new book, "Dream Teams: Working Together Without Falling Apart." Shane is a great storyteller and weaves together fascinating research and stories from music, business, police forces , sports, and the gaming world to provide ways to embrace cognitive friction.

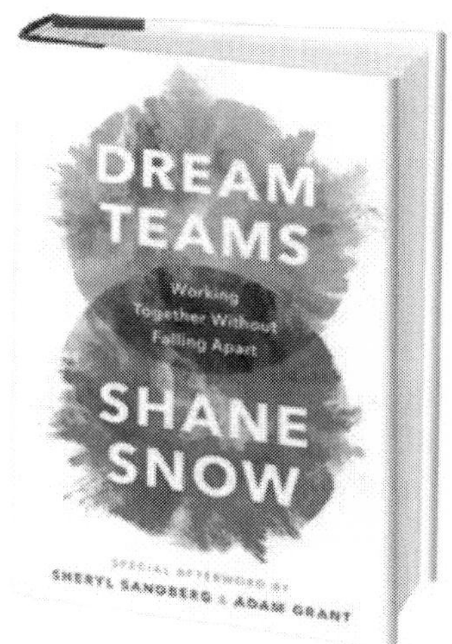

Some of my favorite takeaways:

Cast your teams: "Routine problems don't require much (or often, any) cognitive diversity, while novel problems benefit from it greatly. Based on that do a casting session for who you need on the team. When you take this approach we start to think of our differences as gifts." (HT to Keith Yamashita.)

Bring in more rebels: Having a naysayer in a group shakes up thinking in valuable ways. "Dissenting views by a minority of individuals stimulate the kinds of thought processes that lead to better decisions, better problem solving and more originality," per Dr. Charlan Nement of UC Berkeley. The presence of a minority viewpoint helps groups look at issues "on all sides." In other words, you need people to provoke group think and kick you out of inertia.

Play more: "Neuroscientists have demonstrated that play and laughter can actually change our brains to be less fearful...Playing can physically help the brain to get braver...and make us less afraid of cognitive friction."

Don't value your values too much: Shared values make us more likely to think the same, stop searching for better solutions once we have solutions that work, and add to organizational silence. "Seven out of ten American employees in companies with strong values hush up when their opinions are at odds with those of their superiors," according to research by Warren Bennis at the University of Southern California.

Cultivate intellectual humility "Intellectual humility makes one more correctly judge when it is time to change" and is a predictor for openness to changing important opinions, curiosity, tolerance for ambiguity, ability to detect the validity of persuasive arguments. In other words, a more open-minded culture needs people with intellectual humility.

Activate oxytocin and empathy with stories: "When our brains release oxytocin for a person who is not in our in-group, the bias we have for them disappears. And one of the key ways we can do that is through sharing good stories." This is why it's so helpful for teams to share their personal stories, from hardships growing up to who in their life helped them achieve a dream.

Read more novels: "People who read a book or more per month, the data shows, are significantly more likely to have high intellectual humility than those who rarely read." Stories cultivate empathy.

I highly recommend Shane's book. And don't miss the footnotes.

DO SOME HEAVY LIFTING

Stay in the Swamp

People are fleeing the swamp of synthesis—that terrible, magical, challenging place where we birth new ideas. It is a swamp filled with discomfort where we look at our research and the hundreds of Post-It notes on the wall and search for patterns and insights that lead us to the "aha" solution.

In IDEO's project "mood map" this is the synthesis phase. And as depicted in the map, it is where our spirits are the lowest. This is the hard, hard work of design and problem solving.

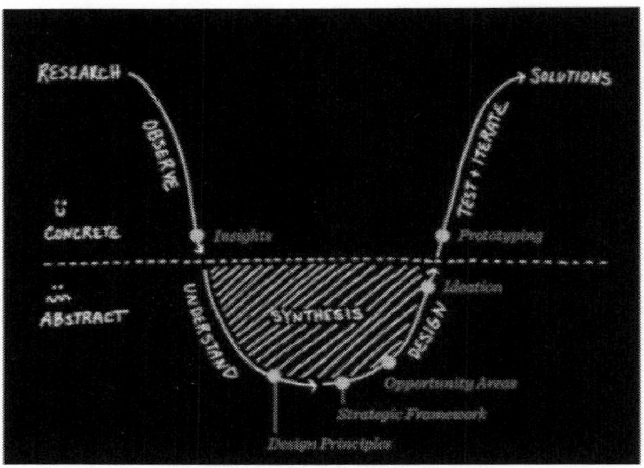

And because it is so difficult, many of us rush through it. We want to get out of the discomfort of ambiguity and uncertainty – and the feeling that we may never get it right.

Is this why we "fail fast"?

When we rush this phase and the initiative turns out mediocre or a bust, we have logical reasons to justify the "fail." Not enough budget for research. Unrealistic deadlines. Customers aren't ready for that much innovation.

The most popular and ridiculous excuse is putting on the badge of honor of "failing fast."

I speak at conferences around the world and this year it seems as though every speaker is urging people to *fail fast.* Aside from this meme starting to sound trite, I have a hunch that a lot of the fast failing is because we spend too little time in the swamp of synthesis.

The beloved Buddhist monk, teacher and peace activist Thich Nhat Hanh has famously written that "suffering is a kind of mud to help the lotus flower of happiness grow. There can be no lotus flower without the mud."

Similarly, suffering through the synthesis phase of ideation is necessary to grow our ideas. There can be no innovative ideas without wading through the mud in the synthesis swamp.

How long to slog, when to get out?

But how do you stay in the swamp long enough, despite the discomfort, and how do you know when it's time to get out? I have no definitive answers here, only observations from facilitating creative teams and doing my own creative work.

First, it's important that leaders understand the importance of the synthesis swamp and that they need to allow time for this phase. Most are too impatient.

A CEO once said her company hired me for "creativity-on-demand." At first, I was honored by the compliment, but then I realized why the company's people were so frustrated and exhausted. Creativity on demand is not sustainable, nor is it sufficient for complex problem solving.

Perhaps we need to educate executives on what to expect. Maybe it's a 30/40/30 model: 30 percent research, 40 percent in the swamp, and 30 percent testing.

My personal challenge when I'm lost in the swamp is beating myself up. "I'm not creative enough. I take on projects that are impossible. Maybe I'm just getting too old for work this intense." You get the gist.

Borrowing advice from Jill Bolte Taylor, author of *My Stroke of Insight*, I speak to my brain as though it's a group of children, and tell them, "Stop it. You're making a racket and not being helpful at all. Whining solves nothing." A little self-compassion and shutting down the "whining children brain" helps me think clearly.

With that clarity, I ask questions like:

- Are we trying to solve the right problem?
- Asking the right questions?
- Looking at the right research? (Often there's too much.)
- Have the right people in the swamp with us? (Groupthink often blinds our ability to fully see.)

Call in your wild pack

I also call people in my wild pack, those friends and colleagues who are what Adam Grant calls "the disagreeable givers." They interrogate my thinking, challenge my assumptions and ask difficult questions that jolt me out of my rut.

Like the synthesis swamp, these wild pack friends make me uncomfortable. And they are invaluable because they stretch my thinking, point out sloppy work, and dare me to take different approaches.

Most of us have plenty of colleagues in our support pack—people with compassion and kindness urging us on—and not enough in our wild pack.

When I was writing my first book I asked a well-known author and brilliant and cantankerous consultant to read the first draft. I was in the swamp and knew something was off. He told me that the first two chapters were so boring and ridiculous that he frankly couldn't stomach reading any more.

I was crushed. And he had done me such a favor. The book eventually won awards, but could have been a disaster if I had rushed it to completion.

Document your time in the swamp

My final observation is to write about your time in the swamp after you've once again emerged from wading through the mud, self-doubt and frustration, and developed an excellent new idea.

What helped you stay in it?

Who and what helped you get through it?

How and when did the aha's emerge?

Keep these notes so you can refer to them the next time you're in that synthesis phase.

And when you're really stuck, try to extend the deadline, turn everything off, go for long walks, and have your support pack give you a little TLC.

No mud, no lotus.

Finding Ideas in Unlikely Places

I'm sitting in the Surgical Family waiting room at Boston's famed Mass General Hospital. People are talking quietly or reading hardcover books. A woman in her 40's wearing black athletic pants and white sneakers is slumped across two chairs, snoring. An elderly man sits upright as he naps, his head bobbing down to the collar of his violet dress shirt.

There are no televisions or bright lights. We're all in a quiet waiting womb.

I, and I suspect the others, are feeling vulnerable, unable to concentrate on anything but our loved one. How will the surgery turn out? Will it be easier or more complicated than the doctors' expected? Will we be able to take our son, daughter, mother, father, wife, husband, sister, best friend home soon or will surprises force a longer hospital stay?

We are all on alert, fully awake and quiet amid the stress of not knowing.

My son was hit by a car two weeks ago while riding his bike back to his dorm in Savannah, Ga. God caught him as he spun from the bike, bounced off the car and kissed the pavement with his beautiful 19 year-old face. He had no concussion, a miracle. The local hospital stitched up the gash on his forehead, and told him to find a plastic surgeon to repair the four broken bones and nerves in his face. So here we are.

Driving by the Charles River this morning at 6 a.m. on our way to the hospital my son turned up the volume of his favorite music group, The Head and the Heart, and mused, "I am so lucky I don't have brain damage from bouncing off that windshield."

This mother bear nodded in fierce agreement. Oh, how lucky we are.

But now I am on edge, waiting for the surgeon's call.

And I am remarkably creative.

Ideas for an education program that I've been wrestling with floated out of nowhere an hour ago. It's like I was taking dictation from some learned person who said, "Here is what people want to learn and what you need to teach them."

"Wait, slow down. I can't write down all these ideas fast enough."

I had been struggling to design this program for over a month and then — BAM! – done in 20 minutes.

Weird ways great ideas find us

When we get jolted out of our usual routines, our brains can say, "Thank you for taking down all those assumption and anxiety barriers. Now we can get you to pay attention to something new."

Sounds crazy. But research shows that when there's less activity in our brain's frontal lobes, we're more likely to come up with an original idea.

According to Dr. Rex Jung of University of New Mexico, inventive brains are less packed and organized and so nerve traffic is slowed down. This gives the opportunity for more unusual connections to be made even if it takes a little while to do so.

Because my brain is much less full than usual as I sit quietly thinking about not much of anything but my son, my brain has been experiencing what Dr. Jung calls "transient hypofrontality." This frontal lobe change has allowed my brain to make new connections, to think more creatively if you will.

There are far better ways to experience this calm brain state than sitting in a waiting room. Researchers recommend running, meditating, walking, and other activities that require us to turn off our devices and noisy brain talk and just be quiet.

My brain was so thoughtful delivering a creative gift to me this morning.

The best gift, however, was the call from the surgeon telling me that my son's procedure was over and was not as complicated as they had expected. Maybe we should play The Head and the Heart's "Sounds Like Hallelujah" on the ride home.

New Growth

It's June 1 and the city garden behind my Providence, RI, office is bursting with new growth. What's fascinating about plants—and organizations—is that so much unexpected and counter-intuitive growth happens at the tips and edges of organisms.

New cellular structures—and ways of working—often happen by chance, emerging unexpectedly in the least likely places. This is emergent innovation, not cultivated by an innovation department, task forces, or forced mandates.

> *"Normally cells enlarge all over the surface. However, in many organisms, there are also specialized cells that grow only at their tip. How the necessary materials are delivered to the growing tip, is largely unknown." Tipping Plant Growth, Universitaet Tübingen, Science Daily, Dec. 19, 2011*

What these "tip growth" areas do need to reach their potential is light.

My invitation to leaders is to allow emerging ideas to develop. Don't over-analyze tiny buds of possibilities, demand ROI, question how they fit with existing policies or spray them with cynicism.

Give people and ideas light. Find possibilities from unexpected sources.

> *"The development of new leaves is triggered by light, a finding that contradicts 150 years of conventional thinking." Plant Biology: New Light Shed on Growth, Nature, July 2011*

LEARN TO BE PATIENT

So Exactly How Long Should You Wait for Change?

The other day I was in a conversation with a long-time rebel who has been tirelessly constructing a radical new work practice for an organization. For years. Except that now he's gotten kind of tired. Perhaps you might even say fed up. His ideas are not really moving beyond the prototype stage and it's been...years.

"People keep telling me that 'Change Takes Time' but my question is: How much time is TOO LONG?"

As a card-carrying member of the "Change Takes Time Fraternity," I realized I had never asked myself that question. Sure, real change takes time but when does that truth become just empty words for the Status Quo to hide behind?

My friend had worked some of this out for himself.

"Many organizations realized the need to move into a different model at around the same time. A decade ago. Most of them now are well underway into making the transition. Some have completed it. But we're still futzing around."

"That's how I know our change is taking too long."

Rebels need to have an idea (maybe even a timetable?) for how long it takes to complete certain types of change in comparable organizations. They need to use this information (cleverly) to establish expectations not just for themselves but also for the organization around them. Because in most change initiatives, the Status Quo remains in fact the most important player.

I can imagine it would be quite effective to let the bureaucratic black belts know what the typical transition time is for comparable change initiatives. Status Quo leaders may not always buy the idea for change but they are quite inclined to support the need to keep to a schedule.

And talking explicitly about how long you expect something to take and "how long ***too long*** is" will also prevent the passive-aggressives in your organization from availing themselves of one of their favorite techniques—using the unmonitored passage of time to wait the rebels out.

Finally, having a clearer framework in your mind to help you determine when change is taking too long will help you avoid rebel burnout. Rebel self-care is essential and yet most rebels are horrible at it. We really do suffer from the sunk costs phenomenon, particularly because our sunk costs usually represent emotional and psychological investments.

Rebels sometimes also need to think about whether they are prepared to stay in their position long enough to see a particular change through. Are you strong enough to hack away at your organization's undergrowth for let's say five years to make something happen? Be honest when you answer that question. Because change takes time.

Don't Worry. Be Gritty!

By now almost everyone has seen or heard Pharrell Williams' infectious, monster song "Happy!" But as I mentioned to our audience at the recent Rebels at Work panel at South by Southwest Interactive, 25 years ago there was another infectious song about being happy—Bobby McFerrin's "Don't Worry be Happy." It was just as popular as Pharrell's monster hit and probably even more infectious.

What kind of advice was that for rebels, I thought. Don't Worry Be Happy. Pretty pollyannish if you ask me! Likely to be met by hollow, derisive laughter. Real Rebels at Work determined to make change are unlikely to just whistle away their setbacks. Instead they'll look for another opportunity and try to learn from their mistakes.

Or as Angela Lee Duckworth—the University of Pennsylvania professor who just won a MacArthur Foundation fellowship for her psychology research—puts it, successful people in any discipline or profession share one common quality—**GRIT**!

In her view grit has two important dimensions; first is the positive habit of being resilient in the face of failure or adversity. But grit without a cause is rather pointless. According to Duckworth, the other half of grit is having focused passions over a long time. Resilience and passions—the two defining characteristics of a Rebel at Work.

Grit clearly is an admirable quality but in my view it doesn't have the happiest of auras. Being gritty conjures up clenched teeth, sweaty palms, and a touch of anxiety. Can a Rebel at Work be gritty and happy? I think so and here are some ways how:

Have more conversations about solutions than about the problems

Too many Rebels at Work, including me, fall in love with the problems of their organization and can't stop obsessing about them. Do an inventory for yourself—I think you'll be surprised by your own positive to negative ratio. Resolve yourself to talk more about solutions than about problems. Just try it sometime. Even think about divorcing your ideas for change from any discussion of the problem.

When you introduce your change idea, don't connect it to what's negative in your organization. Connect it to a more prosperous future. (I know this is the opposite of a burning platform but I've never been too fond of that metaphor myself.)

Do your homework about your ideas for change

There is nothing worse for a Rebel at Work than to introduce an idea only to be informed that the same initiative was tried years ago and failed miserably. Not knowing the history of reform in your organization is a rookie error for rebels. If you think the idea still has merit, by all means pursue it. But being gritty should mean avoiding unforced errors by taking care of the details ahead of time.

Have a trusted ally who can help you be gritty

We've written often about the need for rebels not to go it alone. Having colleagues who support you is essential. But to succeed at being a gritty rebel, it's important to have someone who can talk you down when you're about to go ballistic. Grit means you don't indulge your temper, no matter how good it might feel in the short term. Before you tell people what you really think of them, talk to that trusted ally first. You'll be much happier.

Know how to pivot

Rebels at Work invariably have more than one idea for how their company or agency can improve. Moving on to a new idea when your first one hits too many roadblocks is a much more effective "gritty move" than continuing to pound your head against the organizational granite.

Develop a realistic timetable

How long will it take to get your ideas accepted in your organization? Well, that's a function of both your organization's resistance to change and your idea's distance from current norms. But knowing how long your change initiative might take will make you more patient and help you be gritty and happy at the same time.

Laugh it off

When I think back on some of my rebel episodes now, they're just kind of funny. I wish I could have had that perspective at the time. It would have been healthier for me. Finding the humor in your rebel journey is a powerful way to gain the perspective that will allow you to be gritty. Pick a trusted ally who can help you do that.

Don't worry. Be gritty!

Walk, Don't Run... but Never Stop Walking

"If you stand still, your opposition has the power to knock you down, if you keep walking, they have to follow you," she said. "I'd rather keep walking."

Who's the she who is giving us rebels such great advice? Princess Reema Bint Banda al-Saud. I saw her speak at South by Southwest Interactive two weeks ago. You can watch and listen to her keynote here. I confess I attended her talk thinking that it would largely be a public relations activity for Saudi Arabia. I left mighty impressed with the practical rebel instincts of a woman who is taking concrete steps to improve the role of women in Saudi society. It is well worth the listen.

The "Walk don't Run" part is my riff on what she said. Too often, rebels rush headlong into a change mission, totally psyched by their idea and/or disgusted by the current reality. But as we point out in our book, Rebels at Work: A Handbook for Leading Change from Within, rebels are well-advised to adopt a more measured approach to getting their ideas adopted. Recalibrate your own expectations of immediate and glorious success, which are probably driven more by ego than by common sense. Take your time. But don't stop.

Another great talk full of ideas for Rebels at Work was by Dan Pink who talked about *Fear, Shame, Empathy and More Ways to Change Behavior.* His talk is not available yet for viewing, but there's a handy recap of his major points here. We don't want to brag or anything, but most of his ideas line up pretty good with our advice to rebels.

Use good questions.

Enlist the Crowd.

Give people an easy way to act.

Try stuff. Pilots and prototypes are always preferable to messy and noisy failures.

But there's one suggestion Pink made that frankly Lois and I never thought of.

Make time to rhyme

Rhymes increase process fluency. The message just "goes down better." Think of it like linguistic comfort food.

So now I'm trying to think of some more poetic ways to talk about Rebels at Work. So we could do:

When your boss is a jerk,
You need Rebels at Work.

OK, that's not very charitable. Let's be more positive:

To succeed as a Rebel
Good ideas must you peddle
Of Allies have several
But around bureaucrats be careful

Enough from me. No doubt some of you are more talented than I.

Do You Have a MAC?

Do You Have a MAC?

No, this isn't another installment in the PC/MAC wars. What we want to know is whether you, the plucky change agent at work, know your Minimum Acceptable Change, that first step—or perhaps just a half-step—that you believe will put your organization on the path to progress. I was introduced to this idea just a few weeks ago at a leadership seminar for civil servants in the Federal Government.

We put considerable emphasis on the tactics Rebels at Work need to use in meetings to be successful. For example, rebels should be parsimonious in the time they take to lay out their change ideas, and generous in the time they allot to discussion.

The primary purpose of the meeting is not for the rebel to hear himself talk but rather for the rebel to listen to what others have to say. And that's why obsessing over a "perfect" presentation may not be such a good idea; less perfect presentations provide more openings through which others can contribute. The worst aspect of wonky presentations is how closed they are to other people's suggestions. When confronted with a slide chock full of bullet points, you have a hard time justifying adding one more.

By the way, on the topic of slide decks, have you all caught the clever commercial where a "Bond villain" tortures his prisoner with a slide presentation on his plans for world domination?

But I digress.

Your minimum acceptable change

Another excellent preparatory step you can take before you present your change ideas is to have in mind your Minimum Acceptable Change. The MAC is that action, or series of actions, that you believe moves your group in the direction of improvement, toward goodness. The MAC will be different for each organization. In a sclerotic bureaucracy, the MAC may simply be an agreement to present your idea to the next bureaucratic layer. Because often in bureaucracies, climbing the hierarchy is a type of progress.

Knowing your MAC is useful in a couple of ways.

First, it forces you to be realistic in considering what type of change your organization is likely to accept. It is rare indeed for a Rebel at Work to part the waters at her first meeting. But often that's the only contingency she's planned for so when the audience is not blinded by her brilliance, she has no alternative to offer. With a MAC in her back pocket, the Rebel at Work has a better chance of directing the discussion toward a viable interim step. A rebel I talked to last year told me that she's all about Tiny Pivots, one quarter-step after another that eventually add up to change

Also, having a MAC allows you to avoid unsatisfying compromises. Indeed, your Minimum Acceptable Change can be quite different from a compromise.

In passive-aggressive organizations, compromise is often a type of off-ramp—a way to get the rebel off the road where he can do less harm. So, for example, the clever bureaucratic black belt in the meeting might suggest that you go talk to the Talent staff about your idea, calculating that it will be months before he'll hear from you again. But if you've thought about your MAC, you might be ready instead to suggest a small change in HR practices that could test your new idea.

The MAC strategy works best when everyone can agree that "We need to do something!" Often, we can all see that the status quo is unsatisfactory, but we can't agree on how to fix it. A MAC proposal should have several characteristics:

- The change advocate should believe it would be a useful first step.

- At least one or two individuals who oppose dramatic change should be willing to support it. (This requires some discussions and pre-work before the meeting.)
- It should not require significant changes in regulations or large amounts of new funding.
- Its potential impact should be apparent early on, and the Rebel at Work should have an idea for how to observe/measure it.

During my CIA career, I pushed for the Agency to embrace digital publication methods and move away from the once-a-day "newspaper" format. But that was not my MAC. My initial starting point was a database that we populated with intelligence articles as soon as they were deemed ready. A small number of individuals had access to the database, but they soon testified to its utility. An unanticipated but essential benefit of the MAC was that it revealed many of the other issues that would need resolving before we could embrace digital media.

So before your next meeting, decide for yourself what the best small step forward looks likes. If you don't know where you're going, you'll probably end up someplace else!

The Appeal of Subtraction

You may have heard the self-help gurus talk about how paralyzed people have become by all their stuff, jammed into their houses, garages, storage units. It's overrunning people's lives and making them miserable.

The same thing is happening at work. We have so many programs, processes, special initiatives, goals, strategic mandates, task forces, and focus areas that people are overwhelmed.

I recently met with a company task force that was trying to figure out a way to communicate the brand messages, corporate vision, company purpose, employee values, and four new "pathway to success" programs, all with their own titles and acronyms.

"What should we do," they asked.

"Subtract," I said.

No one cares about all your messages and programs. It's too much. What are the one or two, maybe three things, that will guide and possibly inspire your tens of thousands of employees in their work? What matters for what you're trying to achieve?

The kill your babies message is never popular, but to move forward we have to look at what we can let go — and do far less of.

This is especially important when rebels are trying to introduce big new ideas. Leaders are reluctant to keep adding without some subtracting. There's not enough budget and the "add add add" mentality creates bloated bureaucracy that slows everyone and everything down.

A new library director at a major United States university presented an inspiring vision for what the library could become. The vision, the value, the thinking were superb. The funding needed to realize the vision was $12 million. The provost said, "No."

The library director went back and found a way to cut $7 million from the existing budget. When she went back to the provost he said, "Here's the other $5 million you need."

If your big change idea is stuck in budget approval limbo, ask yourself, "What can we subtract to get the support to do what's most important?"

REBELS IN GOVERNMENT

Top Five Plays of Intrapreneurs in Government

For those of you who participated in our 24-hour Rebel Jam in May, you may remember hearing a presentation from two Deloitte consultants who were just completing a research project on being successful intrapreneurs in the public sector. As you know we rebels go by many names—mavericks, heretics, troublemakers—but one of our favorite labels, if you insist on putting one on us, is intrapreneur. The two authors, Liz Arnold and Shani Magia, have summarized their paper's findings for us to post on Rebels At Work. Lois and I think it will resonate not just with you who work in government but with all Rebels out there.

Intrapreneurs in government

Government intrapreneurs can be visionaries, armed with strong communication skills, the ability to persevere in the face of uncertainty and opposition, and a passion for public service. But even these talents often aren't enough.

Earlier this year, we interviewed individuals who have successfully achieved meaningful change in government. We talked with more than 20 civil servants across the federal government, from the Central Intelligence Agency to the Department of Labor, and collected some of the best "plays" intrapreneurs have used to overcome barriers. Although their strategies are wide-ranging, these intrapreneurs all share a common quality—they are tough and scrappy, reflecting their need to make the best of suboptimal or difficult circumstances.

Find an advocate: Many intrapreneurs face a predicament when they try to make change happen in government: they may find that their initiatives violate existing agency rules and/or they could risk their careers by being change advocates. To help them handle these risks, they can find managers or sponsors in the organization to help navigate organizational processes and procedures to achieve change.

Connect seemingly unrelated dots: Potentially big impacts don't always require the invention of something new. Intrapreneurs often bring ideas from outside their organization to address an unmet need.

Identify Allies: Building a team can be a way for intrapreneurs to gain support for important initiatives. Team members can help generate and validate ideas, and provide and collect feedback. Extra hands help anchor the effort and foster a culture of bottom-up commitment to change.

Look for detours: Intrapreneurs don't let rules get in their way of creating positive change. Intrapreneurs can leverage their networks, build new connections and become salespeople for their ideas to find the detours that make progress possible.

Adopt a "beta" mindset: When introducing a new idea or approach, there can be a tendency to have a "ribbon cutting" to celebrate its success. Intrapreneurs can use pilots to test new ideas, and get stakeholders to buy into new ways of doing work.

What are your best plays?

Different approaches may work better at one organization than another. It's up to the intrapreneur to decide how best to push an idea through. The passion intrapreneurs have to improve the way their organizations work is what drives their creativity—their toughness, their willingness to fight for an idea—their scrappiness. It's what makes them successful.

What strategies do *you* use to create positive change in your organization?

To learn more about our research about Intrapreneurship in Government, please read our study "Intrapreneurship in Government: Making it Work" on Deloitte University Press.

Advice for Rebels in Government

These are difficult times for civil servants. Some have asked us to reflect on what advice Rebels at Work has for federal employees. We offer the following dos and don'ts with a big dose of humility and an even bigger degree of caution. I imagine that everyone will find our advice to be unsatisfactory to some degree: We don't go far enough or we go way too far. But somewhere along the way we hope our readers will find at least one tidbit that helps them.

DO

Do Sharpen your Bureaucratic Skills. If there's a time to get smart about how bureaucracies work, now is it. Whenever there is a new administration, incoming political appointees try to enact procedures without sufficient regard for or even knowledge of existing laws and regulations. It's the DUTY of civil servants, of legacy staff to point out the landmines. Ill-conceived government actions make the US Government vulnerable to lawsuits and public ridicule. They also have the potential to weaken our democracy.

Do Your Job! Don't be so distracted by the current political brouhaha that you do not adequately perform your basic duties. If you are a supporter of President Trump, you do him no favors by putting politics first. And the same goes for opponents. In fact, your partisan views should have no bearing on the performance of the duties of your office. This is the essence of civil service.

Do Write Everything Down! As civil servants you have rights and protections. If you find yourself dealing with a difficult manager, or if you are asked to take actions that you believe are unwise or perhaps even illegal (more on that later!), document as best you can everything that happens. And share the particulars with someone you trust. It's probably unwise to store this documentation on your government computer. Perhaps you can dedicate a favorite notebook to keeping your paper trail. Be sure you don't improperly store or keep government documents and/or sensitive information, however. If management is out to get you, they are sure to use any simple mistakes against you—no matter how innocent or trivial.

Do Monitor your Emotional Well-Being. Right now the hardest-hit government Agency appears to be EPA but employees in all federal departments and agencies will be challenged in the months and years to come. Pay attention to the emotional costs. Forego that extra drink after work. Take a vacation or a strategic mental health day. Don't take it out against your family or friends.

DON'T

Don't Confuse your Partisan Views with your Official Duties. The Civil Service oath demands that federal employees defend the Constitution and faithfully discharge the duties of their office. The US political system would collapse if Federal employees believed their authority superseded that of the American people.

That said, you are well within your rights to argue against a policy decision or an interpretation of the law that you believe unwise or counterproductive. But if you don't win the argument and unless you believe you are being asked to do something illegal, your job is to execute policies regardless of whether you agree with them.

For you own mental well-being, however, it's important to understand your own personal red lines. Under what conditions would I resign from government service? Under what conditions would I go to the Inspector General? Get smart about the whistle-blower provisions in your agency.

Don't Do it Alone. Allies are one of the most critical success factors for

Rebels at Work. There will be many in your workplace who think and feel like you do. Find them and collaborate. Share best practices. Avoid mistakes made by others. You can develop a powerful information network in your workplace.

One Last Thing. We at Rebels at Work often poke fun at bureaucrats. And yet it is often the relentless thoroughness of people making sure all the i's are dotted and Oxford commas removed that preserves due process and the rule of law. As I write Sunday evening, the executive order on immigration is being criticized, even by supporters, for not having been properly vetted and coordinated within the vast US Government bureaucracy.

Take heart, all ye Bureaucratic Black Belts. Your time may have come!!

III

Communicating

Section Highlights: Communicating

There are two big mistakes we make in trying to get buy-in to new ideas. The first is spending way too much time creating the "perfect" PowerPoint presentation, thinking this one document will largely determine whether people will support us. The second is falling so love with our own idea that we blather about what it is and forget to focus on what's in it for others. There's too much "here's what and how" and not enough of "why it matters, especially now."

In the "Make Meetings Useful" section you'll learn the best way to get people's support and what ideas people support.

In "Connect to What People Care About" we share ways to frame your ideas and offer practical communications tips based on persuasion science. (Hint: use a list of "worst practices" instead of best practices.)

Especially important in this section is advice about having difficult conversations. The more important, risky or expensive your initiative is, the more disagreement and push-back there will be. As we wrote in the "Tight Pants" post: a lot of people want to dress up in the matador clothes and hear the applause. But you have to know how to bullfight to be in the ring.

Without being skilled in knowing how to dissent and disagree, we can become judgmental and personal, damaging our work relationships. It's disappointing when good ideas go nowhere. It's tragic when good relationships sour.

CONNECT TO WHAT PEOPLE CARE ABOUT

Are You Solving the Right Problem?

It's discouraging and frustrating to work tirelessly on solving what you think is an important issue and nothing happens.

Despite brilliant thinking, smart teammates, and innovative solutions, the organization never fully embraces the new approach.

There are a lot of reasons why good ideas never get adopted. Sometimes they're not critical to the organization's goals, require too many resources, or scare the managerial keepers of the status quo.

But there's another reason that's rarely acknowledged: **we're trying to solve the wrong problem.**

Defaulting to tactical fixes: a sad, but true story

More specifically, we go after creating tactical solutions – new systems, processes, behavioral ways to do the work – when the real problem is an underlying belief or mindset issue.

It's the old iceberg model: we try to fix the 10% of work that's visible instead of addressing the invisible issues under the surface.

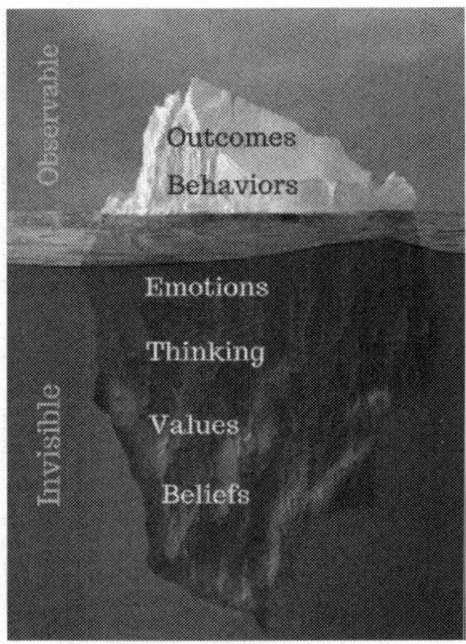

Let me share a story to illustrate.

A few years ago an executive of a large, global company told me that the company's marketing and communications organizations weren't collaborating. Hundreds of people seemed to either being doing slightly redundant work or certainly not working as efficiently or creatively as they could be.

The silos did their annual plans every year and sent them up through their hierarchies to the president, who clearly saw overlaps and missed opportunities.

I was asked to help the two organizations break down their organizational barriers. The immediate goal: develop one integrated plan for the coming fiscal year.

We used Art of Hosting and The Circle Way techniques to identify shared purpose, establish common goals, and have conversations in new ways so that everyone was heard. We created simplified, shared planning templates. There were raucous, collaborative sessions where people worked intently and with good intentions. The thinking was smart; the output was strategic and creative. Great relationships were formed.

But after that one planning cycle, people slid back into their own silos where marketing and communications each did their thing, apart from the "governance" committee meetings that were in reality lipstick on the collaboration pig.

While people gained a new appreciation of one another and the diverse roles in each organization, the goal to create new processes and open communication was a dud.

Uncovering the real problem

After 18 months I was called in to facilitate a session with just four executives – two from marketing and two from communications to figure out "how to fix this collaboration problem."

Sensing that there was a deeper underlying issue, I led the executives through creating an Immunity to Change map to see if there were assumptions and beliefs holding people back from achieving their goal of working together.

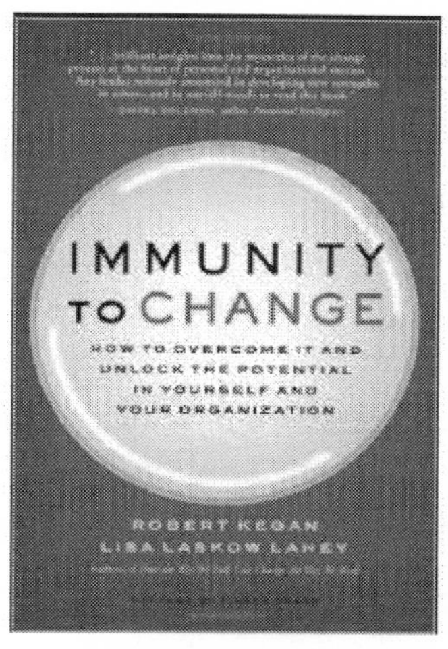

Immunity to Change, developed by Harvard School of Education professors Robert Keegan and Lisa Lahey, is a diagnostic tool that pinpoints individual beliefs and organizational mindsets that make us immune to seeing what's really stopping us from achieving our most important goals. Just as our body becomes immune to disease, our mind can become resistant to certain types of change.

By making these immunities visible you begin to see root causes—and can then focus on solving the right problems.

What was revealed among the corporate executives: the marketing people believed that they and their staffs were much smarter than the communications teams.

That's why marketing didn't want to collaborate. They felt they were the strategic, creative minds and the communications people were tactical and lacking in an understanding of the business issues.

It was a painful session and oddly freeing. Now the real work could begin.

Be a problem identifier vs. just a problem solver

One of the most valuable things Rebels at Work can do for our organizations is to identify the real problems.

While problem solving is valuable, problem identification is foundational.

And one of the most valuable things we can do for ourselves is to identify what might be holding us back from being confident, effective Rebels. Motivation is valuable. Clearing away beliefs that limit our influence is bliss.

* * *

For more information on Immunity to Change, go to Minds at Work, the consulting firm founded by Drs. Kagan and Lahey or read the book, which explains the research on resistance to change, how to create an immunity map, and how individuals and organizations have used the process to unlock what's holding them back from making important changes.

Communicating New Ideas

Most rebels do a great job at bringing passion and enthusiasm when talking about their ideas, which is essential for getting people's attention. In addition to this positive energy, there are a handful of communications fundamentals to master so that people understand your idea, consider its merits, and lend their support.

Show what's at stake

To get people's attention, frame your idea in terms of what people care about. *Show how the idea relates to what they want.*

If there's nothing at stake, if there are no emotionally compelling risks or rewards for acting on your idea, people will probably ignore it. A common mistake we've seen is that people launch into the details of how their new idea will work before doing the much more important work of communicating why it matters so much.

So step one is jolting people awake to understand why your idea matters so much to what's important *to them.* The more relevant your idea is to what everyone wants to achieve, the more likely people will consider it. The more your idea rescues people from a fear or frustration that is getting more acute every day, the more they will consider it. Similarly, *the more widely and/or deeply felt the issue or topic, the more likely people will consider it.*

Paint a picture of what could be

Emotions get people to consider an idea and influence decisions. Paint a picture of how your idea creates a better situation. Expose the gap between how things work today and how they could work. *Make the status quo unappealing.*

Paint a picture of how much better things will be with your ideas in place. You want to make the status quo unappealing and the alternative a much better option, so much better that it will be worth the work to get there. Walk people through how things will work differently with your new approach. Help them *feel* this new way of doing things, evoking a positive emotional response. Remember: people make decisions based on emotions, either the desire to flee from pain or to seek relief and rewards.

Show that the idea can work

Highlight what it will take to be successful and where the greatest risks lie. Show the milestones that will need to be achieved. This demonstrates that you've done your homework and thought through the risks, uncertainties, and practicalities. *People support ideas (and people) that they think will be successful.*

Show the gap between the ideal and where things are today, and briefly *highlight* the milestones for closing the gap and getting to the ideal. Avoid communicating all the details. You don't want or need to drill down into specific details in a meeting where you're trying to get buy in and support. We've seen too many great concepts die an early death because the blizzard of "how it will work" details buried big idea.

You do, however, need to have done your research so that the milestones you present are realistic, doable, and make sense based on how things get done where you work. This makes people comfortable. It helps them see that while anything new is fraught with uncertainty, you have been thinking about the risks and have thought about ways to minimize them.

Build support

Mobilize people to support the idea. *If 10% of the people in an organization believe in an idea, it is highly likely it will be adopted.*

Before doing any formal presentations, talk with people you like and trust at work about the "what's at stake" and "what could be."

Communicating a new idea is about developing relationships, learning from others, asking for their help in making the idea better, and enlisting their support to be able to make the idea happen. A mistake rebels make is thinking that the way to get an idea approved is to present it to the management team, which will either say yes or no.

The way to bring an idea to life is helping people see the value in the idea for them, and asking them to help be part of the effort. Socialize your idea with many people, and work hard to get those one or two first followers who will also take ownership of the idea and start to talk about it. The first followers provide credibility to you and the idea and often can be more influential than anyone in positional authority.

Once the first followers get behind the idea, work together to influence 10 percent of the people in your organization.

Why 10 percent? Scientists at Rensselaer Polytechnic Institute have found that when 10 percent of the people in a group believe in an idea, the majority of the people will adopt their belief.

> *"When the number of committed opinion holders is below 10 percent, there is no visible progress in the spread of ideas. It would literally take the amount of time comparable to the age of the universe for this size group to reach the majority," says Boleslaw Szymanski, the Claire and Roland Schmitt Distinguished Professor at Rensselaer. "Once that number grows above 10 percent, the idea spreads like flame."*

If there are 200 people in your organization, that means you need to get 20 people behind your idea, willing to stand up to the powers that be to say, "We should do this." With just 20 people supporting an idea, it is likely to be adopted. That's not so daunting, is it?

Even if there are 1,000 people in your department or community, 10 percent support means 100 people. Not all 1,000: you need just 100 to get leadership's attention, interest others in considering an alternative new way, and get funding for an experiment.

So create a tribe or community, not just a PowerPoint presentation. Being a rebel is not about being a hero or lone wolf; it's about creating better ways to work with and for our co-workers. The energy, ideas and support from a collaborative group are much more

Be positive and succinct

Show enthusiasm, but don't get so carried away talking that you fail to listen for others' thoughts and good ideas. *How we communicate is as important as what we communicate.*

When you embark on your effort to change that which refuses to budge, act as if success is just around the corner. Be cheerful! Be emotional! Show some enthusiasm. There's nothing less appealing than a dour reformer.

On the other hand, don't let your enthusiasm turn you into a boor. We've all probably sat through presentations where the person drones on and on. There are flow charts, project timelines, quotes, charts so detailed that you can hardly read them, and a running commentary that never stops for ideas or questions. Don't be that person.

And if people don't like what you have to say?

If you've communicated clearly about how to solve a relevant problem and people don't like your ideas, it's wise to pause and assess whether the issue is important enough to keep going, despite the lukewarm reception.

If the answer is, "Yes, this change effort can make a big difference," or "The organization is at risk if it doesn't move in this area," it's time to learn one of the most important rebel lessons of all: how to navigate controversy and conflict.

The Narcissism of Small Differences

"It is precisely the minor differences in people who are otherwise alike that form the basis of feelings of strangeness and hostility between them." ~Sigmund Freud

I've mentioned Adam Grant's new book Originals: How Non-Conformists Move the World. I've done so for the self-serving reason that my Rebel at Work story is captured in Chapter 3. The other self-serving reason is to remind you that Adam is one of the experts we feature in our learning video: Be a Brave, Big-Hearted Rebel at Work.

But this time it's to clue you in to what I consider the most powerful chapter for Rebels at Work in Adam's book—the chapter on creating and maintaining coalitions: *Goldilocks and the Trojan Horse.*

Lois and I have observed that successful Rebels at Work don't do it alone. Often their first step is to form alliances with others; that's certainly what we would recommend. Adam Grant's chapter explores the realities and subtleties of coalitions. His stories and observations not only led me to reflect on past mistakes but also to realize for the first time just how many I'd made.

Adam orients his lessons for building coalitions around the story of the American suffragette movement of the 19th century. Early on the suffrage movement suffered a crippling split when Lucy Stone, one of the first voices for women's suffrage, couldn't agree with Susan Anthony and Elizabeth Cady Stanton on important movement issues, and vice-versa. Among the issues that divided them was the push to grant the vote to African-American men.

Stone supported the right to vote for ex-slaves even if it occurred before woman's suffrage. But not Anthony and Stanton, who were so committed to their cause that they even struck an alliance with a racist opponent of African-American suffrage. Other issues divided Stone from the other two, more-famous suffragettes with Stanton and Anthony holding what could be fairly described as the more extreme positions. Eventually Anthony's and Stanton's disdain for moderation, at one point they allied with the first woman to run for US president—on a sexual freedom platform, cost them supporters and lost them potential victories at the state level. Their organization and woman's suffrage suffered.

Adam Grant labels this tendency of change agents to fight each other as the narcissism of small differences. Another term for it is horizontal hostility.

Research shows (and I bet your own experiences confirm) that groups battling a fierce status quo often disparage more mainstream groups even when they are all trying to make progress in the same general direction.

In politics, for example, political parties can feel more visceral hatred for their potential coalition allies than toward their common opponents. I experienced this firsthand in change efforts I was involved in; many believed I was too willing to compromise just to make some progress.

Striking a balance between your ideals and the need to show forward movement is never easy, but change agents that can find the "Goldilocks" spot enjoy better odds. As Adam Grant writes: "to draw allies into joining the cause itself, what's needed is a moderately tempered message that is neither too hot nor too cold, but just right."

A couple more points in the chapter are worth calling out. Adam recounts how the suffragette leader Lucy Stone and others pursued alliances with the 19th century temperance movement. Although the women backers of prohibition were more socially conservative than the suffragettes, they were able to combine forces to win important victories particularly at the state level.

This story reminds me of how useful it can be for change agents to pursue their ideas through adjacencies. When an issue faces tough resistance, it's often more effective to approach the change indirectly by working first on an adjacent issue.

Adam Grant also makes the case for why rebels should try to turn opponents into allies. This is daunting but worthwhile. "...{O}ur best allies aren't the people who have supported us all along. They're the ones who started out against us and then came along to our side." And why is that? Well, one reason is because a reformed opponent is the most effective proselytizer of others to join our cause.

Adam Grant writes that on her deathbed Lucy Stone whispered four last words to her daughter: **Make the World Better**. I can't think of a better motto for Rebels at Work.

Use the Clothesline

One way to help people see the value of your rebel idea is to show how it connects to the organization's narrative — its reason for being. The uber purpose. The big picture context.

For governments a narrative is like a clothesline, and you hang your policies from it, says David Gergen, communications adviser to four U.S. presidents. Similarly, companies hang its products and services from the narrative clothesline. Doing so helps people understand what's important and how the pieces of the business fit together.

If your idea supports the organizational narrative, people will likely be more open to considering it, or at least paying attention to it.

Narrative as North Star

Narratives are simple explanations. Here are a few examples:

- The narrative of the United States has been about exploring. For Israel it's protecting and defending.
- For Nike it's about serving and honoring the inner athlete. Patagonia is about doing no harm to the environment.
- Southwest Airlines' makes it simple and fun to fly. FedEx absolutely, positively delivers the best customer experience.
- The Rebels at Work narrative is helping corporate rebels *inside large organizations* be more successful in creating positive change.

These narratives can be like North Stars — a fixed point in the sky that can be used to guide decisions, serve as a organizing prompt for telling relevant stories, open up thinking about new products or ways to work.

Narratives can also be a quest. I like John Hagel's view in this Forbes article:

> *"Story chronicles the path and progress of a limited set of protagonists – from the beginning, through the middle, to the end of a story* arc. *Narratives, in contrast, are designed for a growing number of protagonists — many of whom are yet to be defined — who share a common quest or journey that is yet to be fully resolved or completed."*

How do we find our narrative?

To help companies find their narrative, I like to invite people to think of their organization as a cause or movement and speed write a rallying cry, starting with a verb. Or quickly write many responses to the "I believe that ...." prompt about their organization or company. No over-thinking, self-editing or corporate speak. Just ideas, beliefs and aspiration, from the gut.

I've also been suggesting to people that they NOT make this a formal process. Take some narrative possibilities and insert them into casual business conversations. Then into some presentations as a way of setting context to your ideas. See how people react. Ask them questions like:

- Does this help you better understand our strategy?
- Do you more clearly see how this new product line fits with our overall business?
- Can you imagine how this policy falls outside of our focus?
- Does this narrative sound like our company?
- Is this narrative something you like being part of?

See how well the narrative serves you. If it works, quietly seed it so it can grow and serve others BEFORE bringing in committees, copywriters, lawyers or naysayers. Insert it into the CEO's talking points. Use it to frame the next acquisition or product launch. If it helps, then make it better known and part of the company's leadership strategy.

And if it doesn't resonate? Keep experimenting.

Finding a narrative gives your organization meaning.

Showing how your maverick idea can manifest this meaning opens opportunities and helps disarm the naysayers.

Learning from the Persuasion Scientists

Influencing people and decisions is complex, but there's much we can learn from persuasion scientists. This past weekend I read the great new book, *The Small Big: Small Changes That Spark Big Influence,* by Steve Martin, Noah Goldstein and Robert Cialdini.

Here are some highlights, all based on fascinating research studies that the authors explain in the book.

Communicating

Before a meeting or interview, write about a time you felt powerful and/or adopt a high-power physical posture. "High power" people are more persuasive.

Make sure to present your credentials before trying to influence a group. Authorities' opinions dominate people's minds, shutting down cognitive consideration of other factors.

Focus first on the possibilities and potential of your proposal, as potential arouses more interest than realities. Once the attention is focused on the potential, provide supporting information about the benefits, e.g., testimonial, research data.

Admit uncertainty vs. convey over-confidence. A person's expertise, when coupled with a level of uncertainty, arouses intrigue. As a result—and assuming the arguments that the expert makes are still reasonably strong—this drawing in of an audience can actually lead to more effective persuasion.

Similarly, consider using a list of "worst practices" instead of "best practices." People pay attention to and learn from negative information far more than positive information. Also, downside information is more memorable and is typically given more weight in decision-making.

Influencing decisions

Ask people to choose between two options vs. offering just one. Then influence them to opt for your preferred option by pointing out what could be lost if they don't select that option.

Similarly, people make decisions based on context and comparisons. By first presenting an option that people think is a bit too costly, or one that they might think will take to much time, you can achieve the desired impact of making the target proposal seem even more like the "Goldilocks proposal that it is—just right.

Determine whether you're trying to get buy-in or follow-through. If it's getting people on board, make the sequence of steps as flexible as practical and emphasize that flexibility when announcing the initiative. If the bigger issue is execution, give the rollout sequence a very structured order and emphasize how, once in place, the program will proceed in a straightforward, uncomplicated fashion.

Forming relationships

Use someone's first name more often when seeking to influence them.

Identify uncommon commonalities between you and another person, fulfilling people's desire to both fit and still stand out.

When meeting someone for the first time dress at a level that matches your true expertise and credentials. This is in keeping with a fundamental principle of persuasion science—authority. Authority is the principle that influences people, especially when they are uncertain, to follow the advice and recommendations of those they perceive to have greater knowledge and trustworthiness.

Getting commitments

Remind people of the significance and meaningfulness of their jobs, and show how what you're asking them to do is related to that meaning.

To get people to follow through on promises, e.g. I'll bring up your idea in the executive staff meeting, ask how they'll go about accomplishing the promise they've given to you. This specificity helps them follow through.

If you believe that you will encounter resistance with your requests for an immediate behavior change, you might be more successful if you instead ask for a commitment to change at a given time in the future, say three months from know.

Appeal to people's sense of moral responsibility to the future version of themselves.

Improving meetings

Ask people to submit information before a meeting. This often increases the number of voices that are heard, potentially leading to a greater number of ideas generated. Similarly, ask people to spend a few moments quietly reflecting on their ideas, writing them down, and submitting them to the group. Doing this can help ensure that any potentially insightful ideas from quieter members won't get crowded out by people with louder voices.

The person who leads the meeting always speaks last. If a leader, manager or family elder contributes an idea first, group members often unwittingly follow suit, leading to alternative ideas and insights being lost.

If you want to create an atmosphere of collaboration and cooperation, have people sit in a circular seating arrangement.

Creative sessions are often more fruitful when held in rooms with high ceilings.

Building your network

Just ask! People tend to underestimate the likelihood that a request for help will result in a yes. Plus, those who can help often don't offer because they wrongly assume their help isn't needed. Why? Simply because it wasn't asked for.

People who help others but don't ask for favors in return are much less productive than their colleagues. The way to optimize the giving process in the workplace is to arrange for exchange: a) be the first to give favors, offer information or provide service, and b) be sure to verbally position your favor, information or service as part of a natural and equitable reciprocal arrangement. ("I was happy to help. I know that if the situation were ever reversed, you'd do the same for me.")

Provide *explicit* thanks and genuinely communicate your appreciation for the favors done and the efforts made on your behalf.

Who Needs the Soft Skills?

"We think that technology people might benefit from some of the soft skills," an O'Reilly Media executive said when he approached us about doing a video program based on our book, "Rebels at Work: A Handbook for Leading Change."

Carmen and I smiled and agreed, holding ourselves back from being bad rebels and shouting, "Might?? Might?! It's all about soft skills. You can't get any kind of meaningful work done if you don't know how to enlist support, have difficult conversations, build positive relationships with people who aren't necessarily warm and fuzzy, communicate in ways that connect with heads and hearts, and develop personal resiliency so that you can weather those times when things don't work out."

Like good rebels, we calmly acknowledged that there is a need for soft skills if you work with people, and if your work requires you to get support for new projects or introduce new ideas, you need soft skills squared.

Then we got to work creating a program that's like a graduate seminar in organizational dynamics and emotional intelligence, interviewing fascinating experts like Adam Grant, a Wharton School professor and author of *Originals: How Non Conformists Move the World*, Maria Sirois, a psychologist with deep expertise in positive psychology, Paul Furey, a psychologist who coaches business people in how to have difficult conversations.

Some soft skill highlights from the "Be a Brave, Big-Hearted Rebel At Work: Get Unstuck, Find New Perspective" video learning program:

The single most important "soft skill" to develop?

Reduce the anxiety of people you're talking and working with. Executive coach Maria DeCarvalho on how to deliver difficult messages.

The single biggest mistake to avoid?

Creating disruption at work. Focus on developing relationships, not disrupting and alienating people. *Corporate Rebels United's Peter Vander Awera on learning from setbacks and failures.*

What to do when the you-know-what hits the fan?

Lean on your most dominant character strengths, and be more of who you are when you're at your best. *Psychologist Maria Sirois on developing optimism and resiliency.*

How to find the right boss and place to work?

When interviewing probe how open the organization is to people who want to introduce to ideas. Specifically ask: What happened to people who brought up unpopular ideas? What questions are off limits? (Ideally, none should be) What's the biggest problem in this organization that everyone recognizes and no one talks about? *Author and Wharton professor Adam Grant on what to look for in managing the relationship with your boss.*

The amazingly simple way to settle down and not say something stupid when we're becoming emotional?

Say what you're feeling. When we hear ourselves say what we're feeling we settle down and become more rationale. *Psychologist Paul Furey on managing your emotions and anger.*

What is the biggest reason so many good ideas never happen?

We create solutions to the wrong problems. *Maria DeCarvalho walks through the Immunity to Change framework, which helps diagnose the real problem in an organization.*

What would happen if there were no rebels at work?

Insanity. Art of Hosting master facilitator Tenneson Woolf in the Parting Shots video, a free segment with some "best of" advice.

Who needs to improve their soft skills? All of us.

P.S. A recent study in the U.K. found that soft skills are worth £88bn to the UK economy. According to Neil Carberry, director for employment and skills for the Confederation of British Industry, "Business is clear that developing the right attitudes and attributes in people - such as resilience, respect, enthusiasm and creativity - is just as important as academic or technical skills.

Aarrr!! Talk Like a Rebel

If you follow me on Twitter, (@milouness) you may have noticed my link to "The Origins of Office Speak" by Emma Green in "The Atlantic." It not only fills you in on Management Lingo but also serves as a quick tutorial on the history of scientific management and the consulting profession in general.

One theme that runs through this history is the slow realization over the last 100 years by business managers and consultants that human beings are most productive when you treat them as real people, not resources. What a concept!! My favorite quote in the piece was from Professor Joanne Ciulla of the University of Richmond.

> *Attempts at engineering appropriate attitudes and emotions can actually undercut genuine feelings for a company.*

The article got me to thinking whether there is such a thing as Rebel Lingo. You know things that Rebels at Work say when they are trying to win support for their change initiatives that actually have the opposite effect.

As Lois pointed out on our Facebook page last week, it is vital for rebels to paint pictures of where they want to go in a succinct way that appeals to what is most relevant to the executives in your organization. That is not compromising your principles, by the way; this is understanding human psychology and keeping it real.

So here is my short list of phrases rebels need to try to avoid. Do I avoid them all the time? No! As I've learned, most cliches became so because they contained a kernel of truthiness. But as a general practice, Rebels need to talk about specific ideas and changes, not high-falutin' concepts. We welcome any additions to the list.

Burning platform

Call the Fire Department! This phrase was born out of the belief that people will resist change until you give them a compelling reason to do so. But I've learned that what you think is a burning platform is often their sunny beachfront property. The Rebel has to have some compelling arguments to prove that the status quo completely lacks feck. It rarely does. The truth is most people resist ***being changed***...period.

Working group

"Let's form a working group!" is that seemingly innocent phrase that brings the 2+ hour meeting to a close when no one has any other good ideas for what to do next. Managers often resort to the working group tactic as well, which alone should give Rebels pause. Remember: Working Groups are groups that do ***NO*** work.

Ostrich, sand, head, butt

Never put these words together in a sentence. They don't win you any supporters.

Change agent

Never introduce yourself in meetings as a Change Agent. Don't let anybody call you that either. Rebels at Work do not get a 10% cut off the top of all change initiatives. We aren't agents at all. We actually believe in what we are doing.

End state

This always makes me think of Death. Also it reflects an unattractive hubris on part of the Rebel. The rebel's ideas are not the end state of the organization; in a few short years (months) your ideas will be overtaken by much better ones. It is the way of the world. Innovation (another word to use infrequently) is not about a program to implement one new idea or even a set of new ideas; innovation means ***permanently*** removing the barriers to entry for all new ideas.

Think out of the box

Aaargh! Please don't ask people to think out of the box. I once heard a senior leader say that he enjoyed being in a box. It was a much safer place to be.

Paradigm shift

It is a shame that Thomas Kuhn's useful concept is now so tired and overused that its deployment in any meeting immediately chills the air and causes butts to shift in their seats as if perhaps an ostrich were involved. Remember: Change agents use working groups to shift paradigms.

MAKE MEETINGS USEFUL

Meetings: Some Counter-intuitive Advice

Oh, the meeting, that time where you hope you can get through your PowerPoint presentation within the allotted time, have everyone love your ideas, and walk out getting exactly what you want.

Oh, magical thinking. Meetings are never that tidy and easy.

Yet meetings are an essential part of introducing new ideas, one reason we developed an entire segment of our video learning program, Be a Brave, Big-Hearted Rebel at Work: Get Unstuck, Find New Perspectives, to this topic, interviewing the talented Brice Challamel, author, entrepreneur, innovation expert, and a master of running meetings.

Some of his recommendations:

The worst thing you can do in a meeting

Present a fully formed, perfect idea. You'll be tempted to want to shove the idea down people's throats, cautions Brice. Instead introduce your idea as a work in progress and ask people for their suggestions, whereby they become your allies and collaborators. The idea will get better as will your relationships.

The best way to get people's support

Ask people what it would take for them to support the idea. And then listen respectfully to their suggestions. If people feel they are listened to, they will listen to you.

What ideas people support

Their own. The best way to get people to support your idea is to make it their idea. Again, ask for what they think should be included vs. trying to get them to buy into your version of the idea.

How long you should talk

Spend a small time presenting the idea, and leave the majority of the time for discussion about what people heard. This is how you improve an idea and gain support. "It's important to remember that the purpose of the meeting is to gain allies for later," says Brice. It is during the meeting conversations that we're able to do that.

What your PowerPoint needs to be

"Keep it as simple as possible so you have room for improvisation based on what's happening in the room."

When to let go of an idea

"Sometimes it's better to lose your idea and save the relationships," says Brice. "You'll have other ideas, but it may be difficult to repair damaged relationships."

In Defense of Meetings

Many years ago a leadership team I was part of took a personality test that evaluated our styles against four attributes:

- Motivated by Big Ideas
- Motivated by Human Relations
- Motivated by Completing Tasks
- Motivated by Analytics and Method

In the day-long feedback session, we sat with our fellow style peers—the Big Idea people all sat together, those who loved to get things done were all at one table, and so forth. I was sitting with the human relaters—we really liked people. After a few minutes of conversation, each group reported out what they most liked to do in the office and what they hated.

My people-lover group was stunned when the "Get Er Done" folks reported that the aspect of organization life they hated most was meetings. Us touchy-feely types had all agreed that we actually enjoyed meetings.

I remember that day every time someone disparages having to attend meetings.

I most recently heard a young friend of mine do so. His work is technical and scientific and he briefed it recently to a group of colleagues in nonscientific support roles. He described the meeting as a waste of time so I asked him what he believed to be the purpose of providing the briefing to support staff. He thought about it for a second and said, "Well, they're not going to provide me with any substantive suggestions."

"Correct." I said "so the purpose of the meeting is to..."

"Let them know what I do so they understand better the support they can give me." He finished. With that context, he realized he described the meeting as a waste of time because he misunderstood its real purpose – the meeting was not about him as much as it was about them.

So meetings often get a bad rap because participants are confused about their purpose and/or because several of those attending had different agendas.

My friend the scientist was used to sharing with his peers to gather their substantive feedback. But with the support group, it wasn't about substance; it was more about camaraderie and creating bonds of trust and respect. Once he understood that goal, he realized he could be more lighthearted in his approach, sharing fun stories and even bloopers. (Although us people-people think story-telling is always a good communications strategy.)

Some common sense lessons I've learned about having better meetings – perhaps some readers may even grow to like meetings – or at least tolerate them better.

Be clear about the purpose of the meeting—not the written agenda but what's really going on

In general, you should have face-to-face meetings when there's an important human dimension to the issue at hand. And us human-relater types think there almost always are important human dimensions – so that's a real blind spot we have.

But most other personalities in the workforce tend to think things like "the facts speak for themselves" or, much worse, "I already have the answers" and so they devalue the utility of meetings. (And by the way they also overestimate their own brilliance!) And when they do agree to a meeting, they conduct it like a standardized test or a fire drill. (a little more on that later!)

Don't hold lengthy meetings just to update people or gather specific comments

Of course, updates are necessary but I'm sure you've been in work situations where the weekly update meeting is held even when there is nothing to update.

It's better to provide updates, according to business consultant Paul Axtell, as a sidebar to a meeting where some substantive issues are being discussed. And one of the worse types of meetings, I think, are what we called in the Intelligence Community "coordination meetings." Ten people need to sign off on some type of content so they're force-marched into a room where they wait their turn for their five minutes of air time. AAARGH! Often the person who came to the meeting with not much to say ends up droning on in some type of perverse payback for being forced to listen to everyone else.

There are of course many occasions when a group discussion of a topic is useful—the topic is particularly controversial, for example, so everyone on the team needs to hear all perspectives. But determine that beforehand—ask your collaborators if they think it's necessary to coordinate as a team before you put it on the schedule.

Recognize the socializing importance of meetings

I know this is the aspect of meetings that drove my more "efficient" colleagues crazy, but the small talk, the banter that occurs at the start or end of meetings is not trivial. It's when colleagues catch up with each other as humans, when we share some funny story, when we perhaps reveal what's really on our minds. Humans don't establish trust by following orders or reporting out the latest numbers – they learn to trust by getting to know each other.

That's what happens during banter and small talk in the work place. One more point – the conversations that occur as meetings end can be quite revealing. We advise Rebels at Work to pay attention to those conversations—that's when some people may finally mutter what they really think and when introverts who haven't spoken up during the meeting might be more willing to share their thoughts.

Many of the meeting haters and efficiency experts have over the years recommended the ten-minute and/or standup meeting as a way to stop wasting time. I'll concede there are scenarios where such fire-drill approaches are called for—in a hectic environment where every minute really is precious. But my suspicion is that they're used more by managers who haven't thought through the message they're sending.

When you tell your staff that you only have ten minutes to meet with them, you're also telling them that you don't have time for their ideas. It better be a life or death matter for a team member to bring up an issue, and it better be something that can be resolved in a minute or two. What complex, important issue can be resolved in 120 seconds? Not many I know of. We put standup meetings in the same category as "open-door policies" and "no problems without solutions"—management best practices that aren't!

HAVE THE DIFFICULT CONVERSATIONS

Talking About What Matters Most

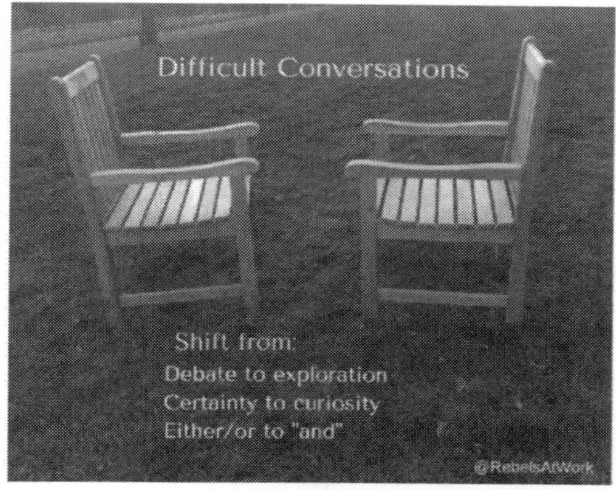

Everywhere Carmen and I speak people tell us that one of their top challenges is having difficult conversations.

One of the best sources for learning to have tough conversations is the Harvard Negotiation Project and the book from faculty members Doug Stone, Sheila Heen and Bruce Patton, aptly titled "Difficult Conversations: How to Discuss What Matters Most."

My biggest takeaway from the book is that we can't change someone's mind in a conversation. No matter how skilled you think you may be. It's not going to happen.

The purpose of a conversation is to create mutual understanding of an issue so that you can both figure out the best way forward. The goal is to genuinely figure out what's important to the other person and express what's important to us. That's how shifts and change begin to happen.

I encourage you to read —no, devour and highlight — this book. It will not only make you more effective at work, your personal relationships are likely improve, too.

Until then, these book highlights will get you thinking in some new ways.

First, understand mistakes and realities

Biggest mistakes

Blaming: it inhibits our ability to learn what's really causing the problem and to do anything meaningful to correct it.

Believing it's their fault: when things go wrong in relationships, everyone has contributed in some important way.

Assuming we know the intentions and feelings of others.

Avoiding the problem is one of the biggest contributors to a problem.

Not preparing, rushing, catching someone off guard.

Not acknowledging feelings.

Important realities

Difficult conversations are almost never about getting the facts right. They are about conflicting perceptions, interpretations and values.

They are not about what is true; they are about what is important.

What happened is the result of what BOTH people did – or failed to do.

Difficult conversations don't just *involve* feelings; they are at their core *about*

The two most difficult and important things are expressing feelings and listening. (And our ability to listen increases once we've expressed our feelings.)

When a conversation feels difficult it's because something beyond the substance of the conversation is at stake for YOU.

People almost never change without first feeling understood.

Don't share your conclusions as "the" truth; explain your thinking.

When conversation goes off track reframe it to focus on mutual goals and issue at hand.

Having a difficult conversation

Prepare

What do you hope to accomplish? What's the best outcome?

Is a conversation the best way to address the issue? (Sometimes what's difficult has a lot more to do with what's going on inside of you than what's going on between you and the other person. So a conversation won't actually help. You've got to do some inner work.)

Plan a time to talk. Don't do it on the fly.

How to start

Reduce the other person's anxiety! Don't put them on the defense.

Describe the issue in a way that rings true for both sides and is free of judgment, e.g., We seem to have different assumptions and preferences for how to accomplish work we both feel is important. I wonder whether it's possible for us to look at the best approaches in view of what we want to achieve.

Explore: their views and yours

Listen and explore their perspectives, asking questions, acknowledging feelings, paraphrasing so the person knows you've heard them.

Express your views and feelings: what you see, why you see it that way, how you feel and who you are. Begin with the heart of the matter for you, e.g., "What is important to me is..."

Problem solve and figure out best way forward

Figure out the best way forward that satisfies both of your needs.

Talk about how to keep communication open as you move forward

Good questions to use during the conversation

What did we each do — or not do — to get ourselves into this mess?

Can you say a little more about how you see things?

What's most important to you about this situation?

What information might you have that I don't?

How do you see it differently?

Were you reacting to something I did?

How are you feeling about all of this?

What would it mean to you if that happened?

How do you see the situation differently?

Help me understand how you would feel and how you might think about the situation if you were in my shoes. What would you do and why?

Facilitating Healthy Dissent

When we corporate rebels disagree, it signals we care about an issue. That we want to wrestle with it to find better approaches.

So why do people so often try to shut us down?

Many people think disagreeing means that we're being unkind and insensitive. Or impolite. (Egads!) "Let's take this off line," they say.

What's unkind to me is pretending an uncomfortable issue doesn't exist when everyone knows it does. There's a tension at work when this happens. Nothing is moving forward, corporate inertia is draining us, and we're becoming ever more skeptical about the cry for greater collaboration.

Furthermore, the longer an issue is ignored, the more frustrated and demoralized people become. Even worse, trust and respect among people erode. And when that's gone, the organization gets crippled.

> *"When someone comes to a meeting and states an opinion or makes a suggestion that his teammates don't agree with, those teammates have a choice: they can explain their disagreement and work through it, or they can withhold their opinion and allow themselves to quietly lose respect for their colleague," says organizational health consultant Patrick Lencioni in his excellent book* The Advantage: Why Organizational Health Trumps Everything Else in Business.

> *"When team members get to choose the latter option —withholding their opinions— frustration inevitably sets in. Essentially, they're deciding to tolerate their colleague rather than trust him."*

More than most, we rebels see healthy dissent as a team sport, where everyone with something to contribute is expected to contribute. If you don't speak up your silence can be interpreted to mean that you agree and have nothing to add.

We view dissent as a way of together getting stronger, like a team preparing to hike Mt. Everest. All the potential issues are honestly discussed and worked through to increase the likelihood of a successful expedition where no one gets hurt. We're fed by the positive energy around these conversations. We appreciate and value what our colleagues have to say.

We also listen fiercely and ask frank questions. It's about inquiry vs. preaching.

But most organizations practice advocacy instead of inquiry in their conversations, say Sue Annis Hammond and Andrea Mayfield in *The Thin Book of Naming Elephants.*

> *"Advocacy is a win-lose form of communication...each person is trying to convince the other that there is only one right answer. Dialogue assumes people see the world differently... each person assumes he or she can learn something new from others."*

Practices for inviting healthy conflict

So what can you do to move from advocacy to inquiry? To help foster healthy dissent vs. angry debates? Here are some suggestions.

Establish agreements: set some guiding principles at the start of a meeting and keep them posted on the wall as a reminder. If someone starts to violate an agreement, bring everyone's attention back to the list on the wall. Here are some guiding principles that I have found helpful:

- Judge ideas, not people.
- Focus on solutions and ways forward; stay away from drama and problems.

- Observations are more useful than opinions.
- Let each person complete their thought; avoid interrupting.
- Ask questions that illuminate, not interrogate.
- Ask questions that are brief and to the point without adding background considerations and rationale, which make the question into a speech
- Respect other people's truths.
- If you want your views to be heard speak now. Not later in backroom side conversations.

Set the tone: Open the meeting by going around the room and asking everyone to respond to a soft but relevant question where there is no right or wrong answer. No one comments on what a person says, just respectfully listens. This helps to put people at ease, build personal connections, make sure everyone's voice is heard, and get comfortable with listening. I recently asked a group about the most creative thing they had done outside of work in the past month. The answers were hilarious, and that laughter set a relaxing, collegial tone to dig into important issues.

Set up what's at risk: Frame the conversation by succinctly stating what's at risk and why it's so important to debate the issue and get everyone's views. This focuses the conversation and reminds people why it's worth their time and honest input.

Make sure you have enough time. Issues worthy of inquiry and debate usually require more than the typical one hour time allotment. One hour meetings are good for updates and touching base. Strategic conversations where we value everyone's involvement need more like three hours, maybe a even a day or more.

Facilitate or use a facilitator. Effective facilitators carefully listen, guide, inject good questions to open up new conversation veins, move people off dead horses, prevent any one person from hogging the conversation, help the group to recover if someone has said something hurtful, and adhere to the meeting agreements. If you are facilitating, know that it will be difficult to participate. As a participant you're focused on the ideas not the meta conversation. Understand what role you'll be playing, participant or facilitator.

Ask the wind-down question. It usually gets to the real issues: About 30 minutes before the meeting is to end ask, "What hasn't been said that should? Is there something you feel we've been avoiding? If we never talked about this issue again, would you feel satisfied that we honestly examined all the important aspects of it? If not, what needs to be said?" Inevitably someone speaks up and speaks the truth and the real conversation starts.

Close with insights: After summarizing highlights and next steps, ask everyone to briefly respond to a closing question, which further respects views and makes sure voices are heard. Possible closers might be:

- How did your thinking on this issue shift?
- What one thing did you find most useful from the discussion?
- What was the high point of this discussion for you?

Rebel at Work or Reactionist?

Last week was the anniversary of Princess Diana's death twenty years ago. The *Wolf Hall* novelist Hilary Mantel remembered Diana in a l ong article for *The Guardian* in which we learned that Diana thought of herself as a rebel. Mantel writes that Diana described herself as a 'rebel,' on the grounds that she liked to do the opposite of everyone else.

And then Mantel makes this key observation:

Throwing a tantrum when thwarted doesn't make you a free spirit. Rolling your eyes and shrugging doesn't prove you are brave... That is reaction, not rebellion.

Oh, I thought. Mantel has put her finger on a phenomenon Lois and I see all the time when we talk to groups about being more effective Rebels at Work. In the question and answer period, we always hear from several people who pose a question that goes something like this.

How do I get people to listen to me when I know they are wrong? When I speak up at a meeting I can see them all rolling their eyes.

Now, thanks to Mantel, I can explore whether their problem might be that they are just Reactionists and not really Rebels at Work.

If you know your Russian history—and who among us doesn't—Reactionist sounds like one of those anti-Tsarist groups. Nihilists, Bolsheviks, Anarchists, and Reactionists. And like all of those groups, Reactionists can sometimes be just as destructive. They often disagree just for the sake of it; no matter what anyone says, they'll take the opposite viewpoint.

It's always easy to find fault with how your boss or your organization is running things. It's much easier to mock a decision than to make one. But you know, that gets old quickly and your teammates will soon just start tuning you out.

I know this from personal experience. During the 1990s at the CIA, I acquired a reputation for being cynical and negative. As one friend commented, "Carmen, I think the only thing that will shut you up is if we all acknowledge that you are right." She had nailed it—I wouldn't be satisfied until everyone acknowledged I knew more than they did.

Let me just say this is not a path to success.

So if some of this is ringing true to you, let me offer a regimen to contain your inner Reactionist. (And none of us is immune to the Reactionist tendency, by the way.)

1. At your next team meeting don't say anything until the last ten minutes. Just listen. If you're a veteran Reactionist, your very silence will shock your colleagues and provide you an immediate tactical advantage—the element of surprise!
2. Because you've been quiet for most of the meeting, no doubt you will have generated a long list of stupidities that you want to comment on. Reflect on that list. If it's particularly long, you can be confident that you are either A) on the worst team of ALL TIME, or—and more likely—B) A World-Class Reactionist, sort of an Eeyore and Cassandra wrapped up in one package.
3. Assess your list of stupidities and decide to bring up only one of them. Obviously it should be one you think is important but more crucially—if you want to repair your Reactionist image—it should be something on which you can offer a constructive suggestion. And something you can frame in a positive way. Perhaps you can say something like this:*I think doing* **X** *will take us in the right direction, and we could build on that by* **insert your suggestion**.

Repeat steps 1-3 as necessary.

IV

Challenges & Obstacles

Section Highlights: Challenges and Obstacles

It's not a question of whether Rebels will suffer setbacks; the only uncertainty is how many challenges and obstacles you will have to overcome. We speak from deep experience on this topic, because together we have experienced just about every obstacle in the book.

One of the hardest things is controlling your emotions when you suffer a setback. Anger is of course a natural reaction, and you need to manage it before it destroys you. Sometimes, we get punished for our rebel ideas, but that time in the penalty box can be an opportunity for reflection and renewal.

Managing relations with your boss is a perennial Rebel challenge. A question we are asked at almost every presentation is what to do when your boss takes credit for your ideas. We have some surprising advice.

Sometimes an obstacle can be avoided if we're just a bit smarter about how we operate. We have some ideas for being a smarter Rebel at Work and for avoiding common missteps.

WHEN YOU SUFFER A SETBACK

Anger: When You're Mad as Hell

Anger is powerful in a good and bad way. It can motivate us to act and it can derail our good intentions and credibility.

Carne Ross, former British diplomat and founder of the Independent Diplomat, quit the British Foreign Service due to his anger over how issues in Iraq and Kosovo were handled by official powers.

The Museum of Modern Art's Paola Antonelli nailed an interview that led to her position as senior curator at MOMA by angrily addressing an interviewer's dismissive statement on design. "Anger can make you do interesting things. Beneficial good can come from positive anger," she has said.

Anger helps us see what we deeply care about, and it pushes us to act on those beliefs.

How anger derails, hurts our credibility

Anger can also trigger us to say and do things that make us say and do stupid things.

Rebel frustrations can grow so acute that we lash out when we and our bosses and colleagues least expect it, surprising everyone, especially ourselves. We feel momentarily victorious finally saying what needed to be said. The outburst relieves pent-up stress. Then we realize that we have damaged ourselves. People have paid attention to our anger, but not necessarily our point.

When someone or something sets us off our heart starts racing, our jaw clenches, we sweat, our mouths go dry, and the voice in our head barks at us like a drill sergeant, "Set the record straight right this minute, damn it. Don't be a sissy. Give it to them."

In a rage we say things that attack. We come across as judgmental and hot headed. When we spew our anger, people usually run for cover or shut down as they wait for us to finish our rant.

Nothing good comes from these outbursts. Most damaging is that our anger gives others the ammunition to discredit us, labeling us as loose cannons, blowhards, short fuses, temperamental, overly emotional, hot headed, immature, unstable, lacking judgment, and maybe even an ass. It is all code for implying not so subtly that we are not a person the organization can, or should, trust.

What a mess.

When you feel you're about to erupt, it's essential to call on behaviors that help you cool down before spouting off. This requires enormous discipline and much practice. While we have gotten better at doing this through years of experience, there are times we fall off the wagon and blow up the bridge.

Let that rage go so that you can respond in a way that conveys your point of view but does so in a way that advances your position or credibility.

Techniques for managing anger

Here are some techniques to practice. See what works for you, and practice, practice, practice. By controlling your anger while also finding motivation from it, you'll be able to act with more credibility, calm and effectiveness. You'll also be more receptive to understanding the real obstacles you need to deal with.

No personal attacks. Never, ever attack the person and use hurtful, rude, derogatory language towards them. Personal attacks cut the deepest and are the hardest to recover from. Go after the issue, but not people.

What's it like to be them? Try to understand what it's like to be the person (or group) you're angry with. What are they trying to protect? What makes them uncomfortable? What are they afraid of? How people talk about something conveys more information than the words themselves. Listen for the emotion beneath the words. This empathy will help neutralize some of your anger and help you see things more clearly.

Find the data: Related to the above point, consider the upsetting idea, opinion, decision or person as a piece of data to be examined. Even if it makes your bile rise, there's something to be understood in why the view is making you angry. Put on your anthropologist hat and try to observe what the real issues are. This calms down the negative anger and prevents you from lashing out. You'll glean valuable insights by taking this approach, and you'll earn credibility by showing people that they can express ideas without someone dismissing them or biting their heads off.

Everyone is right: When angry we often believe we're right, the other side is wrong. No helpful conversations can happen when we hold this belief. Everyone's views (and underlying emotions and threat triggers) are valid. (Unless there is some excellent research proves otherwise. If that's the case, show them the data and get onto objective territory as fast as you can.) If you acknowledge that the other side's view is valid, they are more likely to appreciate that your views may be valid. "Your views on this topic are valid. It is risky to change a process that's been in place for years. Similarly, my views are valid too. There are other types of risks if we don't begin to change this process." This sometimes works, and sometimes doesn't. . But it's a practice worth practicing.

Acknowledge the tension and disagreement: Disarm yourself and the situation by acknowledging that tensions are high and disagreements are real.

- "We're all feeling frustrated and on edge abut this. How about we go around the room and everyone shares what they're feeling in a sentence or a couple of words? No interrupting, just everyone calmly telling us his or her position."

- Or, acknowledge that you're at an impasse and suggest, "We're not making progress because emotions are running high, even those that are unstated but bubbling under the surface. Should we adjourn so we can all cool off?
- "Are there any data or research or subject matter experts we could bring into the conversation to help us see more clearly?"
- "Should we get an objective outsider to help facilitate our conversations so that we can resolve this situation?
- These questions recognize the tension and take an active approach to finding ways to address them. Often people suppress their anger, going passive while the frustration continues to build, increasing the chances of a harmful emotional outburst when you least expect it.

Quarantine your email and your mouth: Impose a 24-hour no-email, no furious phone call quarantine on yourself. Take a walk, get out of the office. If pressed by the other person to respond, say "I have to reflect on this before being able to respond in a helpful way." In other words, quarantine your mouth.

Make a list: Go someplace away from people and write fast channeling your emotion and trying to find answers about what to do next that would help you move forward. Writing while angry cools you down, while also capturing potentially valuable ideas. (My best ideas come when I'm angry or feeling vulnerable. The head turns off, the smart heart kicks in.) Some prompts that have been helpful to us:

- What 10 things worry people most about this idea?
- What 10 pieces of objective data or credible anecdotes would help people open up their thinking around this?
- What are 10 things I can do to move the idea ahead that don't require approvals and meetings with people who oppose the idea?

- What 10 people could I talk to who could help me see a way to move ahead?
- What are the 10 worst things that will happen if I abandon this idea?

Anger will always be present and powerful

Lastly, accept that anger will always be present and powerful for rebels. The secret is being aware of the paradox of anger. It can power and it can derail. Use the power, and find ways to stop yourself from doing and saying stupid things when angry.

We rebels work ahead of most people, so we can get extremely frustrated that people don't see what we see. Acknowledge that helping others see new ways always takes longer than we think it should. Persistence and focus helps, lashing out and biting their heads off does the opposite.

When You're Thrown Under the Bus at Work: Part Two

Thousands of people have read my original post, "Better Techniques for Throwing Employees Under the Bus." The tone of that post was a tad tongue in cheek, perhaps not helpful for people who have been betrayed at work. Here are some some thoughts on what to do if you have been thrown under the proverbial bus.

Don't let your anger lead you astray: First, try not do anything dumb that will further exacerbate the situation and harm your reputation. When we're feeling betrayed, our emotions run wild and dangerous.

Go under the radar for a while: Just as highly public figures like politicians or entertainers often do after a humiliating experience, go quiet for a while. Do work that rebuilds your credibility and doesn't make waves. Learn how to better navigate the organizational politics. (Obviously this doesn't apply if you've been fired.)

Remember that this is work, not your life. People are taking their work more personally than ever, and when work gets too personal people fall apart when something goes wrong. While passion for our work motivates us, we can't let it consume our whole lives. Work is not family, religion or our identity. It is a job. Benjamin Hunnicutt, an historian and professor at the University of Iowa at Iowa City who specializes in the history of work, worries that work is fast replacing religion in providing meaning in people's lives.

> *"Work has become how we define ourselves. It is now answering the traditional religious questions: Who am I? How do I find meaning and purpose? Work is no longer just about economics; it's about identity.*
>
> *Job-satisfaction studies over the past 20 years indicate that people are looking for identity, purpose, and meaning in their work, but very few are finding those things. That's why people are job-hopping, desperately trying to find the work equivalent of the Holy Grail. They aren't finding it because what they're looking for — salvation from a meaningless life and a senseless world — simply can't be found at work."*

In other words, love your work, but always maintain a life outside work that provides meaning and contributes to your identity. Should you get thrown under the bus, you will have better coping skills to bounce back. You are not defined by your job.

Think of the betrayal as a divorce: It's natural to rehash what went wrong and get angry about it. But at some point you begin to get mired in those feelings and get trapped, acting as victim. The other route is to acknowledge the hurt, free yourself of anger and resentment, figure out what you can do to put the issue to rest and move on. Not easy.

Put on an anthropologist hat: Try to look at the situation like a scientist to more objectively understand what happened, and what you can learn from the situation. Eruptions, though painful, can be tremendous learning experiences. We get much smarter from our missteps.

Avoid failure language: Calling yourself a "failure" is unhelpful, and may blind you from learning and recovering from the situation. We creative, innovative types tend to accomplish much, but not without missteps. If your ideas were threatening, or you didn't understand the environment well enough before stepping on a landmine, your actions or behavior erred. But you as a person are not a failure.

Find a new boss: whether inside the same organization, or in a position with a new company. Sometimes you're never going to succeed with a particular boss. You can't change him or her; only find canny ways to maneuver. Is the energy spent on maneuvering a good use of your energy? It might be depending on the opportunities and the organization. Or maybe not. See my previous post on how to find the right boss for questions to ask in an interview.

Getting thrown under the bus is a terrible experience. It may be painful, but next time you'll be so much more prepared.

I also like this thought from author Sherrie Kenyon:

> *"Everyone suffers at least one bad betrayal in their lifetime. It's what unites us. The trick is not to let it destroy your trust in others when that happens. Don't let them take that from you."*

The Rebel Penalty Box

The other day I was having lunch with a friend, a Rebel at Work, and she told me that she was finally out of the Rebel Penalty Box at the office. Immediately I knew what she meant.

"How did you get in the Rebel Penalty Box?"

"Well, actually the year it happened I thought I was doing the best work in my career. I thought I was really getting things done that would make a difference, implementing change. But I guess my boss didn't see it that way. And I received a lesser ranking in my performance review that year."

"Whoa!! What did you do then?" I asked.

"I decided to just go low profile. Just do exactly what was expected of me. And wouldn't you know it, that worked I guess. This year, my performance rating was raised to its previous level. So I guess that means I'm out of the penalty box."

That story was so familiar to me and I bet to most of the rebels reading this post. At some point in your work life you will get a minor penalty or a 5 minute major, and you will need to find a way to get through it without losing your sanity or your rebel core—they're kind of one and the same thing, right?

In my friend's case, it came as a complete surprise—she thought she was excelling at doing the right thing and was jazzed up about her performance. Only to find that, in her case, a change in upper management meant a new definition of success.

My time in the penalty box was longer, I think. Most of a decade. A five-minute major. And I kind of knew it was coming. I wasn't doing the best work of my career. I had let myself become cynical and negative and eventually people just became quite tired of me. I deserved that time in the rebel penalty box.

So, if you find yourself in the penalty box, how should rebels think about it? What can help them get through the period?

Try not to dwell on the fact that it's unfair. Of course it's unfair... in a way. But you're probably in the penalty box because you broke a rule of the organization—either explicit or implicit. In my friend's case she did not factor in the likely behavior of a new boss. They almost always reconsider the priorities of the previous regime—it might as well be a rule. We're not saying don't ever break the rules, although we do think changing rules is a much better strategy for the long term. But just keep in mind that if you're out doing something new, the chances rise that you'll be called for a penalty. It's the risk you run.

Take your helmet off and cool down. In ice hockey, players are advised to remove their helmets so they can release more heat and cool off from the exertion of the game. Not a bad idea for us rebels. The relative peace and quiet of the penalty box can be a great opportunity to think things through, replay the moves you made, and think about your future strategy. In my friend's case, she minded her p's and q's to regain her footing with the new boss. We know some rebels might find that distasteful, but remember that in ice hockey, fighting when you're in the penalty box will probably get you ejected from the game.

Be thankful you weren't ejected. Unless of course that's your goal. Maybe you're so tired of trying to make people listen to your ideas that you've decided to leave. Getting thrown out is your grand fireworks finale. But just be careful how that plays out. Your firing might be the example that sets back change efforts in the organization for years to come.

Look for an opportunity to score when you leave the box. There's no more exciting play in ice hockey then when an aware teammate passes the puck to the player leaving the penalty box. It usually creates a scoring opportunity. Perhaps you can look for a new position where there's more tolerance for new ideas. Or maybe new leadership arrives that's more amenable to change. Having been in the penalty box, the rebel is more likely to observe larger patterns at work that he can begin to take advantage of.

The Rebel Penalty Box Revisited: Avoid Becoming a Bruiser!!

The text below is from our friend and fellow Rebel at Work Curt Klun. He posted it on the Google+ community Corporate Rebels United and kindly agreed to let us repost it over here. You can always tell a good metaphor when others can mine it for additional insight, and that's exactly what Curt did. And just a reminder—the metaphor is not mine but from yet another Rebel at Work.

Olympic/professional players have to expect to endure the box, and from experience, it sometimes feels more like a "hot box" in Cool Hand Luke. While you can also take advantage of the penalty time to add new tool sets for the next opportunity of engagement, I'd recommend using the "down time" to decipher what sent you to the penalty box in the first place, for each set of referees (status quo keepers) have different rule sensitivities and histories.

Did you receive the penalty because:

- you were executing your coach's plan too aggressively and outpaced the system's ability to cope
- you were receiving too much limelight chafing authority in power, overly threatening sacred cows, or clumsily revealing ugly truths;
- you were excessively operating outside your assigned role on the team; and/or

- you forgot that this is a team sport in that change requires official and covert partners and buy-in?

Learn from my burnt fingers, for I have unwittingly ran afoul of all of these offenses. The risk of becoming an unrepentant or repeat offender is receiving the reputation as being a dumb oaf or even worse, "a bruiser" — one, who like a raging bull in a china shop, runs over others towards what they see as their own goals or even intentionally hurt others.

If one receives a reputation like that, the organization's referees will be hyper-vigilant over the most minor infraction in order to perpetually neutralize you. You may even become a disposable hatchet man for other leaders; be marginalized back to a junior league team in Siberia, where you will do no harm; or be slated for rejection from the team, when politically convenient.

Our goal is to return to the ice with a greater understanding of the environment and a refined set of change finesse tools. Finesse is that much more important in order to keep the organization moving forward, while leading change. Surgical finesse is especially vital, when the sensitivities of others and risks appear that much more dire. For instance, when we have been asked to change the corporate engines while flying full throttle and at altitude.

Also remember that as much as we love the mission and the organization that we serve, that we operate in a system of official and unofficial rules, and that there are consequences/opportunities, when we work the edges of these rules.

The one thing to always keep forefront is having a keen knowledge of what the rules are, the reasoning and equities behind the rules, and how one needs to behave in order to work the seams and processes to advance the organization in the right direction, while avoiding being called out for a penalty or doing harm.

In honing such skills of finesse, we will hopefully increase success, engender trust, and open opportunities for advancement into positions of greater influence.

Jill Abramson: Rebel at Work?

Most of our focus at rebelsatwork.com is on employees trying to make change from below. They have it rough and don't have many resources to help them. But we recognize that not infrequently the Rebel at Work can also be a manager, even a leader of an organization.

Steve Jobs, of course, comes immediately to mind. Often leaders try to prod their organization to a better future by painting a vision of a new business model only to struggle to push everyone there.

When I was in the Intelligence Community trying to do something similar, I would often refer to the Keystone Kops to illustrate our challenge. In the silent Keystone Kops one-reelers, there's often a scene where a truck of Kops in pursuit of dastardly criminals turns a sharp corner and several of the Kops fly off. My goal, I would tell people, was to turn our sharp corner but keep everyone on the truck. We're all getting there together.

Easier said than done. Last week the New York Times fired their editor, Jill Abramson, and charges have been flying around ever since as to the reasons why. I don't know why, of course, but I was struck by the analysis provided by another prominent female editor, Susan Glasser, editor of Politico Magazine.

In her article, Glasser posits that Abramson, and the editor of *Le Monde*, who was also forced out last week, were caught up in the strong backlash that can often beat down a leader trying to take their obstinate organization to a place it doesn't think it needs to go.

Glasser can't prove her conjecture, but she writes convincingly of her own predicament when she tried to lead the *Washington Post* to a digital future.

Glasser's description of what confronted her is painful to read.

> *"In the course of my short and controversial tenure in the job, I learned several things, among them: 1) print newspapers REALLY, REALLY didn't want to change to adapt to the new digital realities; 2) I did not have the full backing of the paper's leadership to carefully shepherd a balky, unhappy staff of 100 or so print reporters and editors across that unbuilt bridge to the 21st century;"*

She goes on to write:

> *"I have no wish to relitigate a painful past episode by writing this, except to say what I learned about myself: It was not the right fight for me, and I didn't really have the stomach for waging the bureaucratic war of attrition that is the fate of the institutionalist in a time of unsettling change. I had always chafed at the constraints and processes and internal politics of a venerable and proud place. Was I the right person for that job at that time? Clearly not, and I was happy once the ordeal was over, and grateful for the support I received from so many people. I learned that I liked to invent more than reinvent, that it is a better fit for me to create something new than to try to save something old."*

That last sentence brought tears to my eyes. **I would rather create something new than try to save something old.**

This realization occurs to so many rebels just at the moment they decide to give up. But I suspect most rebels, perhaps even Glasser, are not being completely honest with themselves. My guess is that they really would rather save, revive something old, but that the personal cost of it just becomes unbearable. Or they are removed because when it comes right down to it, too many people expect change to be easy and not controversial. Even when rebels get "top cover", it is flimsy and easily blown away by the complaints from those who will not be moved.

Much of the criticism of Abramson reminds me of our now almost infamous Good Rebel, Bad Rebel chart. Lois and I have mixed feelings about the chart because it oversimplifies a complex subject. Many rebels have qualities on both sides of the spectrum. And sometimes rebels do have to employ the black arts. Lacking the ability to change minds, they focus instead on trying to create immutable facts on the ground. Rebels who are not also leaders almost never succeed this way. And what we've learned once again is that being a rebel leader doesn't guarantee success.

DEALING WITH THE BOSS

How to Find a Good Boss

"I like the concept of rebels in the organization—and am a rebel. It has not always been with a positive outcome. Do you have any ideas on how to find the "protectors" within an organization for Rebels? Specifically, in a job interview how would you know if this potential boss would give the rebel freedom and protection?"

Here are some questions to ask in a job interview to assess whether the person might be a good "rebel" boss:

What is the organization trying to achieve?

This reveals whether a clear organizational purpose exists. When there is a clear purpose, rebels have a much easier time because they can link their new ideas to how they support the big organizational goal or purpose.

What's possible that hasn't yet been done in this [field|company|organization) or What are the greatest opportunities for the organization?

This helps you see if the potential boss is a forward-thinking idea person. (Aside: A corporate rebel recently told me that her new CEO told the top execs to stop thinking about new ideas and focus their energy on executing his strategy (which they disagreed with). That no-possibilities boss is losing some of his best talent.)

What do you especially like about the organization's culture and work environment?

The response to this will uncover whether the person is positive and appreciative of the strengths of the organization, or a Debby Downer who defaults to problems and negativity. From my observations, positive, optimistic bosses are more open to—and appreciative of —rebels.

What's the best assignment/project you've ever been involved with? What made it so fulfilling?

Does the person most value implementation or creating new things? This idea helps you understand what makes the person tick. Rebels need a boss who veers more to the creating new things mindset.

How do you support people who question approaches that may no longer be effective and see alternative ways to do things?

How a person answers this will be more telling than the words themselves. Is the person comfortable with the question? Does the answer flow easily and naturally—or does it take a bit to find the words? Does it sound like the person truly values truth-telling idea people? Or do you detect some annoyance? Does the response indicate that people regularly bring up ideas and the boss has a genuine and comfortable way to support those people and ideas?

Lastly, look around the work environment. Do you sense a lot of energy and positive buzz? Or is there a hushed, disengaged feeling? I know this is a bit touchy-feely, but the physical environment speaks volumes about whether it's a place rebels can thrive.

After walking around the offices of a big ad agency last year, I instantly knew the company was *not* steeped in creativity. It was too quiet. People were heads down in their cubicles. There were few fun things tacked around cubicles and common spaces. Sure enough, eight months later I heard the agency had lost three big clients.

Ask your potential boss good questions, and find time to walk around.

Why Bosses Say No

"There's no money in the budget for that" is the most common management response to new ideas. The more creative or risky the idea, the quicker our bosses' "Sorry, no budget" reflexes.

We walk away thinking, "Well there's no sense on pushing that idea forward. There's no money to fund it."

But here's an important truth:

Money is rarely the real reason ideas get shot down.

Six common reasons bosses say no and what to do

1. **It's just not that important:** When an idea helps an organization accomplish something that's important and valued, that idea gets funded and approved. Many very good ideas get rejected because they don't support what the organization most cares about. So show how your proposal supports what's most valued.

Consider: Do you know what's most important and valued? What's appearing on the agendas of management meetings? What new buzz words are creeping into conversations? Do this homework before you start socializing your idea. We've seen funds appear almost magically when an idea addresses an issue deeply important and relevant.

2. **I can't understand what the "it" is:** Sometimes new concepts are so foreign that people just can't figure out what we're talking about. As the idea creators we easily "get" the concept, and make the mistake of thinking

that other people will instinctively understand what it is and how it benefits the organization.

Consider: Use an analogy to help people see how the idea is the same and different. When Bill Taylor and Alan Webber had the idea for Fast Company, they pitched it as putting Harvard Business Review and Rolling Stone in a blender and pressing the on switch. What is your idea like – and how is it different?

3. **Timing out of kilter:** Your boss may love your idea and say no because the timing doesn't fit with planning cycles. If you start lobbying for an idea in November but plans and budgets are finalized in September, you're out of luck for a while.

Consider: Learn how decisions get made and the timing of decisions and budget planning. Work with the system.

4. **Where are the best practices?** Innovative concepts are just that – innovative and emerging. They haven't been done before and involve risk and complexity. Alas, many people are extremely uncomfortable approving new ideas unless they can be backed up by best practices or controlled experiments. Without having some sense of certainty, people reject the idea. It's just too risky.

Consider: If you can find supporting case studies or best practices, use them. If not, consider using the Cynefin Framework to engage in a conversation about the context of your organization (or the customer environment) and the implications of that context for making decisions. For example, if people agree the operating environment is becoming more complex, they are more likely to support novel approaches and acknowledge uncertainty.

5. **I don't like the idea.** There will be times when your boss just dislikes your idea for all kinds of rational and irrational reasons, and doesn't know how to tell you. So he asks you to do more research, puts off your meetings, and says things like, "Let's keep this on the back burner." The tough thing about this stall tactic is that you keep your hopes up and become more and more

frustrated. It's the equivalent of the movie, "He's Just Not That Into You."

Consider: if you think your boss is having a hard time giving you frank feedback, help her by asking questions like, "On a scale of one to 10, one being highly unlikely and 10 being very likely, how likely is it that this idea will get approved and funded in the next year?" (Ratings take the emotion out of discussions and give you useful data about intent.) Or say, "It looks like you don't like this idea and you'd like to be able to tell me that. It would help me if you'd say it directly."

6. I love the way things are. Some people just love the way things are and want to preserve what they think is working. They're not so much opposed to your idea as they are in love with the status quo.

Consider: If you suspect your boss is in love with what exists, ask him, "Where do you see value in changing how we operate today? In what ways do you think this new idea could make us more effective?" If he thinks everything is going well and sees little value to changing, you have some important data. You can either build support around and below your boss to keep the idea alive. Or you can accept that he's never going to budge and either drop the idea or go to work for an organization that values what you value.

Emotion trumps logic

Remember that most decisions are based more on emotion than logic. To get to "yes," find out what people yearn to be able to achieve (aspirations) and acknowledge the risks and how you'll minimize them (fears). Aspirations and fears are a common paradox. Opportunities lie in the contradictions.

Lastly, manage your own energy and reputation. If the boss hates your idea and sees absolutely no value in pursuing it, you might not want to pursue it. At least not in his/her organization.

When Your Boss Leaves

Readers of ***Rebels at Work: A Handbook for Leading Change from Within*** keep providing us with ground truth and new insights about life as a rebel at work—many of which we wish we had included in our book. One of my favorites is this lament from a reader who is a longtime rebel at work. When a new boss took over his unit, he got the distinct impression that the new boss wasn't fond of his work suggestions. As this reader wrote,

I feel like I'm being told to go sit in the corner and shut up!

Although it shouldn't be this way, in most organizations rebel fortunes are tied to the personality and management style of a boss. As we discussed in our first book, understanding your boss and gaining credibility are the first things rebels need to do. Life as a change agent is hard, and it gets even harder if you don't have a plan and an order for your actions.

When your boss changes, you almost certainly will need to start over. New leaders are likely to be at least a bit insecure and therefore reluctant to continue activities they're not comfortable with—i.e. they consider uncertain and/or risky.

Don't assume your new boss won't have issues with what you're doing. She will and it's your job to gain her confidence. In our reader's case, he senses that his boss is not comfortable with the "creative ideas that spill over into other domains than the one I'm technically responsible for."

And that brings up another interesting dimension of being a rebel at work. Sometimes you're shut down not because you have ideas for changing your own particular job, but because you have the interdisciplinary skills to offer ideas to help other parts of the organization.

Rebels at Work are often constrained by one-dimensional job descriptions and dysfunctional stovepipes. Rather than encourage individuals to contribute on issues they're passionate about, many organizations prefer employees to stay in their own lanes. They do so so they can hit targets and have predictable results, but their "success" comes at a price: disengaged employees and unrealized potential.

IMPROVING YOUR APPROACH

Mistakes Rebels Make or Why Changing the Status Quo Misses the Point

I was just reading someone's profile on Twitter and I noticed they were all about "changing the status quo." And it just struck me. Changing the Status Quo is not the goal. The goal is actually to travel in the best direction possible, whether in your life, or in an organization. (I think there is rarely — never? — a single RIGHT direction.)

So when a rebel talks about her goal being Changing the Status Quo, she is confusing the means with the ends.

The ends, the positive motivation, is to go to a better place. This often requires you to weed out unhealthy growth, add better soil.(guess who was gardening yesterday!) And sometimes, yes, replanting the entire garden.

Rebels unnecessarily alienate the supporters of current realities, many of whom actually love the Status Quo, by framing their efforts as tear-down projects, rather than as new construction.

So resist framing yourself as a destroyer of the Status Quo. Be a builder of the new! Who knows, you may even find there are parts of the Status Quo you can still use.

Do Something

Innovation managers from two Fortune 50 companies got together a few weeks ago and the conversation devolved into just how frustrating internal barriers are to getting anything substantive done.

Yesterday nurses from a prestigious Boston hospital group talked about patient care and the conversation turned to how impossible it is to improve health care because vice presidents are making decisions without any input from the people working directly with patients. In other words, the nurses.

These conversations can be pretty intense. There are enormous barriers to getting things done inside large organizations.

But talking over and over again about all the obstacles, politics and bureaucracy doesn't help make anything better. Nor does it make us feel better. Dwelling on what we can't do saps us.

I asked the nurses what they had suggested to the vice presidents. In what ways could the nurses be part of the VP discussions about important decisions affecting patients?

Silence.

The nurses are so stuck in thinking that the "hierarchy is the hierarchy" that they hadn't even considered proposing possible solutions.

"What if," I proposed, "you suggested that the nurses and VPs get together every three months to discuss the issues and talk about different scenarios to consider? Maybe you suggest doing this type of collaborative session twice as an experiment to see if it provides more value. If it works, it continues. If it doesn't the VPs can go back to their old ways."

Wishing that things were different is a waste of time.

Similarly, one of the Fortune 50 innovation managers finally said, "Aren't we wasting time wishing things could be different. What if we recognize how it really is and work on a success plan based on that reality?"

People across industries are frustrated with how hard it is do change things at work. The opportunity for all of us is to create possible solutions — regardless of our title or "rank" in the hierarchy — and suggest ways to test them out.

And maybe a way to get started is to NOT to focus on "disrupt the industry, change the world, innovate the business model" kind of ideas.

Sometimes big change starts just by getting the right people together — like hospital administrators and nurses — to talk about the real issues.

> *Magical thinking may lead people to believe that their thoughts by themselves can bring about effects in the world or that thinking something corresponds with doing it.*
>
> Andrew Colman, Dictionary of Psychology

Rebels at Work Revolt at Nike

The breaking news of women at Nike revolting and forcing change is a case history in how good Rebels at Work succeed.

First some backstory.

When women at Nike brought their concerns to managers who they were supposed to be able to trust, they were ignored. When they went through formal HR processes to report harassment and unethical behavior by male colleagues, HR also ignored them. While many executives were aware of the problems, they "looked the other way."

So the toxic work environment continued and women were repeatedly passed over for promotions by less qualified men, publicly demeaned and called things like "a stupid bitch," sexually harassed, and excluded from being part of an inner circle of male decision makers.

But a couple of months a go a small group of women banded together and revolted. Six top executives have resigned in the last month, the brand's reputation is tarnished, and the CEO is under pressure.

Using "good rebel" practices to revolt

While our "good rebel/bad rebel" chart is not definitive, it has helped us spread the word over the past eight years on how to make change in large organizations even if you don't have positional authority. Here's a look on how Nike women put some of these practices to use.

Bad Rebels	Good Rebels
Complain	Create
Break rules	Change rules
Me-focused	Mission-focused
Problems	Possibilities
Alienate	Attract
Energy-sapping	Energy-generating
Assertions	Questions
Pessimist	Optimist
Point fingers	Pinpoint causes
Worry that...	Wonder if...
Obsessed	Reluctant
Source: Rebels At Work	

Attract support, do it together: The first rule of all effective change is to not go it alone. But rather create your own Rebel Alliance, just as the women at Nike did. There is power in numbers.

Overcome reluctance: Like most Rebels, these Nike women revolted reluctantly. They loved Nike enough to tackle an ugly, pervasive problem and a group of powerful men. But there was fear about retribution from male executives and hurting their reputations. Few of us gleefully want to rebel. Rather, it's a duty.

FOR vs. just against: According to Amanda Schebiel, a former Nike employee, "No one went to just complain. We went to make it better." Rebels don't just complain. They want to create solutions to problems that are affecting the success of their organizations and team mates.

Get evidence: To get attention, Rebels find data and proof to back up their claims. The Nike women covertly surveyed their peers about whether they had been the victim of discrimination or harassment. Once the CEO received that survey data, several top executives "resigned." Numbers count.

Demonstrating the magnitude of an issue with data helps make the issue real in ways that are more difficult for executives to discount.

Change the rules vs. break the rules: The Nike Rebels didn't want to break any rules. They wanted to create new rules, oversight and diversity commitments that would allow everyone to flourish at Nike, not just the cabal. They wanted Nike to live up to its mission and values.

Rebels forcing companies to address problems

We recommend reading the excellent investigative reporting on the Nike revolt by New York Times writers Julie Creswell, Kevin Draper and Rachel Abrams.

It's a story all too familiar to many Rebels at Work.

And it is a story that reminds us of the power of people who love their company enough to band together, get the data, persevere and be heard.

> *"The kind of sweeping overhaul that is occurring at Nike is rare in the corporate world, and illustrates how internal pressure from employees is forcing even huge companies to quickly address workplace problems." Women at Nike Revolt, Forcing Change At Last, The New York Times, April 29, 2018*

Rebel for the Soul of Government

"Please don't tell rebels like me to abandon organizations that clearly need them, and thereby abandon the public those organizations serve."

A city government manager sent an email last week challenging the point in the Managing Conflict chapter of our "Rebels At Work" book that "if your values are far removed from those of your boss or organization, you have a stark choice—suffer at work or leave."

Here are his views, which are inspiring and informative.

Real rebels embrace conflict

"I agree values-based conflicts are the hardest types of conflicts to address and they will produce some suffering for the rebel and all around... But should we just assume that a government agency should be left to its own devices when its values decay or become misaligned with their public mandate or do we have a duty, especially as rebels, to do something about it?

"I've facilitated, nurtured, and instigated positive organizational culture change centered around perceived values-based conflicts. Values-based conflicts can be remarkably constructive. They're a shortcut to camaraderie that fails to materialize through decades of strategic, wise, fearful, or polite avoidance of these issues.

"They produce highly efficient relational synapses of trust in critical relationships. What's more, people's values (distinguishable from priorities) are often less at conflict than we or they believe.

"The only way to discover that in any specific time and place is to talk about it; i.e. experiential learning. This is the conversation bad bosses fear most, as they should. The worst bosses have values that are deeply immoral by any standard.

"Avoiding these matters through rebel "self-deportation" ensures a lost organization will never rediscover its collective soul from within. "

Resiliency as antidote to suffering

I'm thrilled that this person has the moral motivation, relationship skills, and resiliency to work through values-based conflict.

While much is taught and written about organizational values and conflict management I'd like to see more people develop a capacity for resiliency. Resiliency practices help you keep going, find meaning in the often long and political process of creating change, and see the good in government agencies—even on days that can feel like you're lost in a bureaucratic hairball.

Without the capacity to stay resilient, rebels often suffer, becoming bitter, angry and not the best versions of themselves. And then they serve no one well—not their organizations, not their family and friends, not themselves.

That's when they need to leave.

The quest for one more day

A senior policy innovation adviser at the U.S. Department of Defense recently told Carmen that one of his goals is "one more day."

"If I can get talented people to stay one more day working for the government, I'm succeeding," he said.

So much attention is focused on national political campaigns.

The people who are making a real difference are these rebels in government, working to make sure agencies deliver on their mission and values.

Oh rebels, please, please, please stay just a little big longer.

V

Resilience for Rebels

Section Highlights: Resilience for Rebels

"Can you tell us more about resilience and self-care? Fighting mediocrity and bureaucracy takes such a toll. How do we keep going?"

These are some of the most popular questions we have heard from Rebels during the past 10 years.

So much so that I (Lois) became certified in Positive Psychology, learning evidence-based practices that help Rebels stay strong mentally and physically, bounce back from setbacks, and adapt to less than ideal situations.

In this section we share our favorite resilience practices. Cultivating resilience is a practice, much like yoga, tennis, golf, or meditation. You never achieve perfection. But the more you practice, the more adept you become.

We also look at four habits highly-effective Rebels seem to share: optimism, self-compassion, joy and being true to one's beliefs.

Lastly, we talk about courage. Most people equate courage with bravery and heroic acts. But the psychology research has found that there are four traits in courage: perseverance, honesty, enthusiasm and bravery. We might not be strong in all of them. That's why courage is a team effort and not an individual act of heroism. Our strength lies in acting together, each of us bringing different ingredients of courage.

Not surprisingly, working with courageous, positive people is infectious, which further strengthens our resilience. We won't ever achieve all of our goals, but we just might be able to look back at our efforts and say, "We learned so much and developed such great friendships."

CULTIVATE OPTIMISM, SELF-COMPASSION, & JOY

Even More Faith

Carmen has often said that "Optimism is the greatest act of rebellion."

Optimism is also a decision.

To look at setbacks as particular to a single problem, temporary circumstances or person.

To consider what needs to be learned or done differently to solve a problem or advance an idea.

To act versus sit on the wishful sidelines.

To keep going.

To support and help kindred spirits.

To remember when you have been successful to know that you will be successful again.

Pessimists blame, eschew responsibility, and give up. Research shows that they also do worse at their jobs and are eight times more likely to get depressed when things go wrong.

All emotions are contagious.

But positive emotions — faith, optimism, appreciation and joy — attract support and inject a spirit of being able to achieve more and go farther than seems possible.

Here's to choosing more optimism and more faith in possibilities.

They are the emotions that carry new ideas forward.

Optimism Lifts

What advice do you wish someone had given you earlier in your career?

"Don't climb, lift," said veteran analyst John Bordeaux in his Rebel at Work story.

There's much to take away from this advice. One question might be, "What allows us to lift?"

Optimism lifts. Skepticism requires climbing.

I remember my first week on a new job talking with a team of discouraged people, demoralized because their client was unhappy with their work.

"Let's try to show the client how much we're accomplishing. How about we change the monthly report formats and list everything that we've accomplished each month in bullet points, right at the top," I suggested.

"Yeah, right," said Cindy. "What happens if we don't achieve those kinds of results?"

Though I had only been at the agency a couple of weeks I was optimistic that we'd be able to achieve more, especially if we changed a few approaches to the work.

"If we do these two things every month I really think we'll be able to report some results that will make the client happy. Let's just try it for a couple of months and see what happens."

This optimism accomplished two things. The team didn't resist my new ideas, although they were contrary to the way most teams did things at the company, and the team did in fact achieve results that surprised them and the client. Someone genuinely believing they could succeed lifted the team, and they achieved more than they thought possible.

Optimism has a powerful influence on people. It helps us to take a chance, do something new, invest in an alternative approach.

This is not about chirpy, fake platitudes and those motivational "Dare to do the Impossible" posters posted on bulletin boards near the lunchroom. I'm talking about adopting a mindset focused more on possibilities than problems.

In a world where the voices of the skeptics and naysayers seem to shout the loudest, we optimists quietly and persistently keep going. We do so because we believe that our idea is possible. We see the reasons why it can work and the value it will provide. We follow our passions, know and use our strengths, are open-minded and open-hearted, and we often reflect about what is working and where we can do things differently.

Sure we fall back and get frustrated, too. Big time. But it's how you respond to setbacks that influences how likely you'll be able to find the energy to get up and continue on.

How optimistic people achieve more

Attract supporters. People prefer to be part of teams that believe what they're doing is achievable. They also get energy from being around optimistic people, so they like to be on your team.

Get the ear of more people. Even if people don't agree with our ideas, they are more willing to listen to us and have a conversation.

Self-motivate themselves. When you believe something is possible it motivates you to stay with the idea, keep gathering information, ask questions, get input, think how to improve on it. Doing this makes the idea even more likely to succeed.

Perseverance with less stress: Perseverance and determination are easier to sustain when you have an optimistic attitude. Make no mistake that being a rebel at work is stressful, but a positive perspective can make it less exhausting. Optimists ride the possibility wave to keep motivated. Pessimists tackle persistence and determination by pushing a rock up hill. People want to surf with you. Pushing heavy objects up steep hills, not so much.

Trigger contagiousness. Positive ideas get talked about. Ones that connect with rational and emotional desires hop on the word of mouth train. "Here's a way we can do our work faster, easier, safer, with more fun, and with much fewer headaches." Sign me up to help.

The science of positivity and optimism

The science backs up these views on optimism.

Dr. Barbara Fredrickson, a scholar in social and positive psychology and author of Positivity: Top-Notch Research Reveals the 3-to1 Ratio That Will Change Your Life, has found that positivity opens our minds and hearts, making us more receptive to ideas and making us more creative. Positive emotions help us to discover new skills, new knowledge, and new ways of doing things – and to recover more quickly when things don't go well.

She suggests that we try to achieve at least a 3:1 positivity ration.

> *"This means that for every heart-wrenching negative emotional experience you endure, you experience at least three heartfelt positive emotional experiences that uplift you," Dr. Fredrickson explains. "This is the ratio that I've found to be the tipping point, predicting whether people languish or flourish."*

You can't force optimism and positivity, using insincere, gratuitous gestures and words. That will backfire. You have to really feel it and mean it. No platitudes and smiley faces. People see right through that.

In fact, the subtle difference between positivity and optimism is action, according to Elaine Fox, a psychologist at the University of Essex in England and author of a book on the science of optimism, "Rainy Brain, Sunny Brain."

> *"Optimism is not so much about feeling happy, nor necessarily a belief that everything will be fine, but about how we respond when times get tough," she writes. "Optimists tend to keep going, even when it seems as if the whole world is against them."*

Optimism practices

Use new words. If something doesn't pan out, refrain from calling it a "failure," or worse, saying "I failed." Sometimes things don't work out. The idea may be too risky for the organization. You piloted a concept and the data indicated it wouldn't achieve enough of the right results. The thinking was sound but the investment costs were far greater than the likely returns. You get the picture. If we use failure words, we label ourselves and our efforts in ways that diminish the likelihood of trying again, or of people supporting us again. We rebels are idea people. Some ideas will work brilliantly, others not so. We're not failures. We're thinkers and experimenters.

Hang out with optimistic people. Not the Pollyannas but realists who see what's possible. Creators vs. complainers. Avoid the Debbie Downers and Negative Nicks wherever possible. Including in your personal life.

Picture it. Envision how people will feel and be better off if you're successful. Keep this image clear. Present this image when taking about your project so people are reminded of the big picture benefit. Ask an artsy friend to make an image of it, for you to use when you have to make a presentation about the idea. Or find a metaphorical image that inspires you.

Try to work on things that interest you. This isn't always possible but when we're determined it's interesting to see how we can shift assignments and responsibilities, especially when we can demonstrate why the work we WANT to work on is important to the organization.

Tune out. Though we rebels tend to have insatiable curiosities, there are some things we should stay away from. Like people who over use fear and anxiety to get attention and manipulate feelings. Hysteria clouds perspective and balanced thinking.

Do one scary thing a year. Something that interests you but you find intimidating, as in "I don't think I could ever do that." Or, "I'd be way out of my league if I took that course." "What would I say if I agreed to give a speech like that in front of those people?" The thing about doing one scary thing a year is that it builds up your confidence. You will almost always find that you do better than you think you could, or you were welcomed warmly by people you don't usually associate with. The benefit? Your optimism increases. You believe that more is possible.

Turn to learning: When you hit roadblocks and frustrations turn to learning and questioning. "What could I learn that would help me figure this out? What's beneath what's going on here?" Questions open you back up to possibilities and restore optimism. Don't stay parked in dead ends.

The Commitments: Self-compassion, Wild Packs, Finding the Good

"The most insightful conversations about leadership are not coming from leadership conferences," I tweeted after reading some uninspiring Tweets about the leadership presentations at the Global Drucker Forum in Vienna.

The irony wasn't lost on me that I had just wrapped up facilitating a leadership retreat for women executives. Not a conference. No experts. No thought leaders. (Geez, I hate that term; it's so 1990s. Just like a lot of assumptions about leadership that we Rebels at Work detest.)

Instead, it was a time for these CEOs, CFOs, and COOs to reflect, have honest conversations with one another, quietly consider what they might want to let go of, and frankly and often boisterously wonder what they might want to do very differently.

I suspect that perspectives shifted because these women had the courage to go deep into themselves and not simply assess their "performance" from the safe context of titles, labels, board assumptions and financial measures. (Another aside: performance seems like another outdated work word. How about contributions instead?)

I've led this type of retreat many times this year, in many parts of the world, for people in many kinds of professional fields and industries. Every individual comes away with different priorities. But three practices especially resonated this year.

More self-compassion

The first is the need for greater self-compassion.

"I am so, so tough on myself" is a recurring theme. (Especially among women and those who self-identify as Rebels at Work.) Our drive and ambition often become internal demons. These nasty demons hold our brains hostage, blinding our ability to see clearly and sucking away our positive energy. We become too self-critical and judgmental.

When we practice self-compassion the demons go away – or at least get quieter — leaving us with more positive energy and a clearer view of our work, according to Professor Kristin Neff, author of *Self-Compassion: The Proven Power of Being Kind to Yourself.*

Self-compassion is not self-absorption, self-pity or being selfish. It is simply treating ourselves kindly, as we would treat a good friend. An interesting research finding I like to share with skeptics: self-critics are less likely to achieve their goals.

Find the good stuff

The second theme is appreciating what IS working well.

In Positive Psychology there is a practice called "hunting the good stuff," where you write down three things – however small — that went well in the day, rather than defaulting to what went wrong. This daily practice of noticing positive experiences builds gratitude and optimism. We begin noticing the good more than all the problems that need to be solved. (Side note: The U.S. Army uses this practice as part of its Army Resilience Training.)

In addition to doing this as a personal practice, I suggest teams do this at the end of the week. Everyone simply shares the three good things about her/his work week in your online community or via email. As the week wraps, you see what you collectively have accomplished, which is always more than you realize.

Run with your wild pack

The third practice most leaders commit to is their wild packs. (Thanks to branding consultant Jeffrey Davis for introducing this phrase to me.)

While most of us have supportive friends in our lives, it's harder to find those who challenge our thinking and assumptions, inspire us to take risks, urge us to take creative leaps outside our comfort zones. These are the people who stretch us because they care about us. We don't necessarily get "atta girls" from them, but we get intellectually and creatively challenged.

Wharton professor Adam Grant, author of *Give and Take: A Revolutionary Approach to Success,* says that disagreeable givers are some of our most valuable colleagues at work. And, I would suggest, as friends.

"Disagreeable givers are the people who, on the surface, are rough and tough, but ultimately have others' best interests at heart," Grant says. "They are the people who are willing to give you the critical feedback that you don't want to hear—but you need to hear. They play devil's advocate. They challenge the status quo. They ask tough questions."

The 2019 big commitments: self-compassion, looking for the good every day, and embracing people who bring out our wild and wondrous selves.

Wiser, wilder, more joyful

As for me, I'm committing to practices – and people – to help me become wiser, wilder, and more joyful. The more joyful part seems especially rebellious for me because it seems almost too pat or superficial. But then I remember the research that says positivity and joy open up our pre-frontal cortex to better see possibilities.

I'm also committing to helping people break the cycle of old-boy, alpha leadership so that more people can work in togetherness cultures. Where every voice is heard and valued, and where we respect intent and contribution more than titles and status.

Wishing you a season of joy — and the courage to commit to one practice that will make you a more brave-hearted, compassionate Rebel at Work.

Human Skills

Tom Peters @tom_peters · Aug 18, 2013
If I see the term "**soft skills**" one more time I'm going to barf. Those skills are the true HARD skills--the ones that effectuate results.
30 150 47

Many of us hate the term soft skills—as legendary business expert Tom Peters tweeted five years ago.

Rebels at Work think a lot about these skills—and know they're not soft at all because if we don't master them, we fall flat on our faces and butts. The recognition that kindness, patience, openness, etc. are productive traits in the workplace is a step forward, but something still doesn't sit right with me. While I've been in Texas the last two weeks helping out my 83-year old mom, I've noticed how many of the skills I need to do right by her are the same skills I need to do right by my colleagues and teammates. Whether we're 23 or 83, we need and want to:

Have agency over our lives: As my mother's range of activities narrows, it's awfully easy for me to assume she can't do a particular task. But my "condescension" only makes her cranky and frustrated, and less likely to try. It's the same dynamic in the workplace. When your colleague detects you don't think they can do something, they usually don't.

Be treated like an individual and not as a cliche: I've gotten into this horrible habit of saying, when my mom is despondent, "What's your problem?" This does not please her. And it shouldn't. Because I'm not reacting to her specifically in the current moment; instead I'm treating her like a cliche. I made similar mistakes in the workplace. I remember one colleague who called me on it one day: "Carmen, I hate the way you say 'U-huh' after every point I make. I know that means you're not really listening to me." That brought me up short! Listen to yourself in the workplace. Do you have pet phrases that you use with certain individuals, verbal tics, that you deploy automatically every time you deal with them? Stop doing it.

Enjoy our lives and have fun: It's hard for my mom to find things to smile about these days. Our conversations too often focus on what's not going right; we rarely chat about what's still good. But every once in a while I remember to make a joke or find the funny, and we both feel the room brighten. I am reminded of a boss I had early on in my career at CIA. He stayed in his office most of the time, and only left it to criticize someone on the team. We scattered like pigeons in the city. Don't be that person!

We have a horrible tendency to segment our lives, to think we need to act one way with our families, another way at work, and yet another way with strangers. And that's how we come up with stupid concepts such as soft skills. We don't need no stinkin' soft skills. We need human skills.

All the time...

Everywhere...

With everyone...

Oh, Those Joyfully Rebellious Role Models

First, he would laugh at the craziness of what I was telling him. Because it seemed I went to him when I was in the thick of something messy.

Then he would offer thoughtful advice. No preaching. And then at the end of our talks he'd often tell me that this would be another great adventure.

Frank, my former client and friend, was joyfully rebellious.

His infectious positivity motivated so many of us to do more than we thought possible.

To take chances, laugh at the inanities of corporate politics, have a difficult conversation we kept dodging, learn more, dig deep to find the answers we needed, and to have fun along the way.

A few years ago, I called Frank to thank him for all that he had done for me over the years, and to update him about my labor of love helping Rebels at Work. "Well, that's really different for you. Tell me more."

I called to express my gratitude to him, and then he told me what he had learned from me. Really? Such joy from a simple act, and an example of advice from Archbishop Desmond Tutu and the Dalai Lama from their book, "The Book of Joy: Lasting Happiness in a Changing World. "If you want more joy in your life, focus on others."

Frank McGonagle died a couple of weeks ago at 89. He lived a long life full of adventure and helping others, despite personal tragedy. (An interesting factoid: he coined the "You can pay me now or you can pay me later" slogan.)

Models of joyful rebellion

People like Frank who have contributed so much are often joyfully rebellious. Not angry, fearful, stern, mean or arrogant.

Think about some joyfully rebellious public figures:

- Nelson Mandela, former president of South Africa
- Ann Richards, former governor of Texas
- Director Spike Lee
- Writer/performer Patti Smith
- Carmen Medina, my Rebels at Work partner and former CIA executive
- Archbishop Desmond Tutu
- Tip O'Neill, former Speaker of the U.S. House of Representatives
- Herb Kelleher, founder of Southwest Airlines

Why have so many used "beloved" when talking about these people?

My hunch is that their rebellious joy has infected us to keep going, to know we can do more, and to appreciate those moments of pleasure along the way.

We don't have to be miserable as we work our work.

Last year at the Savannah Film Festival actor John David Washington was asked what it was like to work with Spike Lee on the film *BlacKKKlansmen*, especially the KKK scenes.

"Spike always showed up on the set full of exuberance," said Washington.

Maybe the most rebellious thing we can do in our current world environment of fear, dissent and anger is to show up with more exuberance and joy.

Here's to joyful rebellion, helping one another, and being lucky enough to find role models like Frank along the way.

The Best Environments for Rebels

"Good" work environments that support creativity, adaptability, change and resilience aren't just about psychological safety, inclusion, management trust, or purpose. A whole lot of it is also about the physical environment of our workspaces.

Our physical environment affects our mindsets, our moods, our behaviors. Bright, colorful environments with plants and natural woods make us feel optimistic, creative, calm, open to possibilities. Sometimes even joyful.

So why do we have to work in such drab work environments? Why don't we rebel for offices that boost our energy and our open-mindedness?

I'm not talking big-ticket Silicon Valley office makeovers, but simply taking a more considered approach to our workplaces. More intentional color. Better lighting. Less junky, cluttered stuff. More plants.

Here's why.

Research on physical work environments

Over the holiday break I went down a rabbit hole of reading research about how workplace physical environments affect our emotions and behaviors, and even signed up for an applied color class at RISD. There's a lot of research into interior design psychology, color psychology, biophilic design, environmental psychology, neuro-architecture and geeky publications like the Journal of Environmental Psychology and the Academy of Neuroscience and Architecture.

I also read the fascinating new book *Joyful: The Surprising Power of Ordinary*

Things to Create Extraordinary Happiness by Ingrid Fetell Lee, former design director of IDEO, the global design firm committed to creating change through design.

Some highlights on how it effects behavior:

Color = more alert, friendly confident: People working in bright, colorful offices were more alert than those working in duller spaces, according to a study of nearly a thousand people in Sweden, Argentina, Saudi Arabia and the UK. They were also more joyful, interested, friendly and confident.

Daylight improves energy, mood, blood pressure: Increasing exposure to daylight reduces blood pressure and improves mood, alertness and productivity. Employees who sit near windows report higher energy levels and tend to be more physically active both in and out of the office. In a study of elementary schools, students in classrooms with the most daylight advanced as much as 26 percent faster in reading and 20 percent faster in math over the course of a year. Hospital patients assigned to sunnier rooms were discharged sooner and required less pain medication than those in rooms with less light.

Too sterile or too disorderly = anxiety, negativity: Disorderly environments have been linked to feelings of powerlessness, fear, anxiety, depression, and exert a subtle, negative influence on people's behavior, as do overly sterile environments. Natural environments, on the other hand, tend to put people at ease. Employees working in environments with natural elements have reported 13% higher well-being and 8% more productive. Another showed that working in close proximity to plants improves concentration and memory retention.

Ceiling height matters: Low-ceiling rooms are best for focusing on the details of a subject or object and high, lofty ceilings are more conducive to abstract styles of thinking, brainstorming, creative solutions, and zooming out to get a bigger perspective, according to experiments by Joan Meyers-

Levy, professor emeritus in marketing from the University of Minnesota's Carlson School of Management.

Humdrum feeds hunger: "In our humdrum environments we live with a sensorial hunger, and without any other means to satisfy it, we feed it," says Ingrid Fetell-Lee. She suggests that our drab work environments lead us to snack more to fill sensory voids.

Easy change for change makers?

I showed Ingrid's TED talk video, Where the Joy Hides and How to Find It, during a recent one-day workshop on change and resiliency for women CEOs. They were mesmerized.

"A lot of change is hard, hard work," several executives told me that night at dinner, "But we can find money in the budget for paint and lighting. We can physically make our offices more conducive to change."

Yes, we can.

So, while the hard work of changing outdated systems and practices takes considerable time and resources, maybe we can at least create physical work environments that reduce stress and nurture optimism and a sense of possibility.

Low cost, high return.

Let's not suppress our thinking and depress our spirits in muted taupes, beiges and browns. These colors, per researchers, elicit seriousness and reliability as well as a heaviness and lack of innovativeness. They are boring, old patriarchal colors.

Growth and change thrive in bright, vivid environments.

Creative Expression: A Holy Resilience Practice

When forms ask for my religion I write "creative expression and kindness." Which always makes harried receptionists smile. But my response is thoughtful, not sarcastic.

Kindness is obvious. "Do unto others as you would have others do unto you."

Creative expression is a different kind of holy. It's about caring for our own spirit. And in doing so, becoming more resilient.

One night in my early 30's I found myself in a hotel room in London so sick and feverish that I could not move. Couldn't get to the bathroom for water. Couldn't lift the phone to call down to the front desk. This wasn't flu sick, this was scary high-fever, delirious sick.

As I lay in the twin bed, my pajamas soaked through in sweat, I started praying with the only part of a prayer I could remember from a childhood without much religious education, "In the name of the Father, the Son and the Holy Spirit. In the name of the Father, the Son and the Holy Spirit."

In my haze I had this epiphany, "Oh, the Spirit is me. I'm praying for my own spirit for help. Not those just other Gods."

The next morning, I was fine. It was weird. After such a fever I thought I'd be sick for a couple more days. Or at least be exhausted that morning. Nope. Rested, ready to go to work.

That's when I started to believe in this spirit of mine, and began to explore ways to get to know it better.

The spirit knows

A definition of religion is a "belief in a superhuman power." For me, my spirit is my superhuman power. It's not rational and logical like my brain. Yet it gives me pleasure, heals hurts and helps me figure things out in a way my analytical brain cannot.

The way I tap into that spirit is doing creative things and expressing myself creatively — writing, art, dance, improv, storytelling slams, cooking. And from these small practices I've noticed that:

Writing helps us understand.
Art helps us see.
Dance and music help us feel.

Just slam the words down

When I was living temporarily with my mother as she was dying I wrote a blog post every day to stay sane and track what was happening. I'd share the daily updates — some hilarious, some so sad — with family and friends to keep them posted. I read them aloud to my mother at night, which opened up beautiful conversations.

During a difficult time in my marriage I took the advice of my writing teacher Ann Randolph: "dare to bare," and wrote about the time my husband had to give me an enema.

Oh boy, did I bare all. In the writing I saw love in a new way. And I realized how my husband's kindness and selflessness was something uncommon and to be grateful for.

People often tell me they want to write a book about their life. Most don't really want to do the work to publish a book. They just need to write down their stories for themselves. To understand what the heck happened.

Slam down the words. Even just for 10 minutes. That's all you need.

If you have a good, nonjudgmental friend, ask him or her to listen to you read your words aloud. Speaking what we write is a way to honor what's in the words, and often remove some shackles. For me, that can be more rewarding than publishing a book.

A peek into our subconscious

Visual expression opens other channels, giving us a peek into patterns and subconscious thoughts, much as some people find in dreams.

I take photos of things that capture my attention. Sometimes I mash up photos in collages. Other times I doodle. I always bring hundreds of postcards to my work with executives to give them a more accessible language to express where their organization is stuck and what they want to be able to do.

Every once in a while, I look at my images and wonder what they're telling me, what they need from me. Some years the woods call me. This year I've noticed photos of gates, windows and doorways. Time for new possibilities and things to explore and learn?

Let's dance

But my favorite form of creative expression is dancing. This is from a woman who had been relentlessly teased by family for dancing like a spaz, totally uncoordinated and unable to follow dance steps.

On Sunday mornings I do Journey Dance, which is a form of ecstatic dance. (Our group reverently calls it Church Dance.) No rules or dance steps. Just great music and dancing to your own groove.

Some mornings my dancing looks more like skipping, twirling, or arms wide open welcoming the world like the opening scene of Maria in "The Sound of Music."

I often find myself unexpectedly laughing. This past Sunday tears just crept up and I wept. I am not the type to cry in front of people, even family. We New Englanders are adept at keeping that emotional stuff tamped down. But the sadness and anxiety that is very real in my life right now needed a place to show up.

The music was Seal singing "Both Sides Now" at Joni Mitchell's 75th birthday special. Turn that up loud, close your eyes, and sway. Oh, my loving soul.

Creative expression helps us become more resilient

Creative expression in all its assorted forms helps us heal, understand and find pleasure in our lives. It is a great gift accessible to all of us, all the time.

We are all creative.
Deeply spiritual.
Full of grace.

I wish you the courage to express you to you.

BEYOND BRAVERY: COURAGEOUS TRAITS

Amplify Courage

Courage helps us challenge what no longer works, fight for better ways, achieve more than we thought possible and overcome all the stress and unexpected land mines that are thrown in our paths.

How do you become more courageous? These four strengths amplify our courage. The more you use and develop them, the stronger they become.

(They are based on the groundbreaking research and classification of *Character Strengths and Virtues* by Drs. Christopher Person and Martin Seligman.)

1. **Perseverance:** finishing what you start; persevering in a course of actions despite obstacles.

2. **Bravery:** Not shrinking from threat, challenge, difficulty; speaking up for what's right even if there is opposition; acting on convictions even if unpopular.

3. **Vitality:** approaching life with excitement, entusiasm and energy; not doing things halfway or halfheartedly; living life as an adventure; feeling alive and activated.

4. **Integrity**: speaking the truth but more broadly acting in a genuine and sincere way; being without pretense; taking responsibility for your feelings and actions.

Reconsidering Superheroes

This post is dedicated to health care rebels working on the front lines; it is an abbreviated version of Lois' speech at the Home Care Alliance of Massachusetts' 2017 Innovation and Star Awards ceremony.

I had dinner last week with a good friend who has worked as a hospital executive for 30 years. When I told her about today's event, she started raving.

"These people working in home health care are amazing," she said. "The stress, the uncertainty of one day to the next, the never knowing when budgets are going to be cut, the seriousness and complexity of patient issues. I'm telling you these health care professionals are some of the bravest people in the world. They are heroic, real life super heroes."

I told her I disagreed.

In the face of fear or danger anyone can be brave.

Health care professionals are more than brave. You are courageous. And courage is one of the most important virtues in our world. Maybe more important now than ever before.

There are four traits that make up courage:

Honesty: speaking the truth, acting in a genuine, sincere way, and taking responsibility for your own feelings and actions.

Perseverance: sticking with what's important and getting things done despite obstacles.

Vitality: bringing enthusiasm and energy to how you live. Not doing things half-heartedly. Feeling alive and optimistic.

Bravery: not shrinking from threat, challenge, difficulty or pain. Speaking up for what is right and acting on your convictions even if they're unpopular.

Courageous people do what is right. They willfully resist taking the easy way out. They rebel against complacency and mediocrity. They keep going when most people give up.

Courageous people inspire us to be better versions of ourselves.

And this room today is jam packed with courageous people.

Honesty, perseverance, bravery, vitality. These are the traits that make us courageous. We all have these innate traits, according to psychology research. And the more we use these traits, the greater our courage becomes.

Getting out of Crazytown

But let's not pretend there aren't those days when stress sucks the energy from us. People quit. Budgets get cut. A patient's family gets emotional and confrontational. Administrative paperwork follows you home. Your car blows a tire and your child is sick and you can't get to work. Your sister gets a bad diagnosis. The basement floods and there goes the vacation money. Your life feels like Crazytown.

Anybody here ever felt like they were in Crazytown?

No one feels particularly courageous on those days. Most of us feel downright pissy.

The big question is: How do some people quickly bounce back from stressful situations and stay positive and optimistic—while others become negative, complacent, or, even worse, think of themselves as martyrs? Why do some people thrive despite life's inevitable obstacles?

They practice resiliency.

Resiliency is simply defined as the ability to cope with stress and rebound quickly. It's not something most of us are born with. We have to consciously develop it.

Four favorite resiliency practices

While everyone in this room knows the value of eating well, sleeping soundly and exercising regularly, there are four other resiliency practices I'd like to share with you.

They've truly transformed my life, helping me quickly adapt and bounce back during those personal and professional Crazytown periods.

Three good things/hunt the good. Every night write down the three things that did go well during the day. Doing this helps us see the good in life, even on the Crazytown days. As importantly, it helps us look for the good every day, developing a more optimistic, positive mindset. Which, by the way is contagious.

Self-compassion/being kind to yourself: No one is harder on ourselves than ourselves. We are our toughest critics. On those tough days, I'd suggest you think of the famous Otis Redding song, and try a little tenderness. For yourself.

When our good friends are stressed and feeling down, we're there to offer them kindness and compassionate advice. "You're too exhausted to think. Go home and sleep for 12 hours and things will look differently when you're rested," we might say to her. Why not give that advice to ourselves?

Appreciating your work mates: Appreciation is the single greatest motivator at work, according to Dr. Adam Grant of the University of Pennsylvania. Not "have a great day" balloons or rah-rah parties. (Though some days those can be so much fun.) I encourage you all to make time twice a year, or better yet once a month, to tell your team mates what they do that makes your work so much better. Giving and receiving appreciation lifts our spirits and fills our tanks with enormously positive energy.

Be in awe: No matter what's going on in our lives, we can stop and marvel at some small wonder in the world. My husband has Parkinson's Disease and today he was off. My worrying lizard brain was starting to act up. I went outside and looked up at the sky finally clearing after last night's vicious thunderstorms. The clouds looked magical. For a couple of minutes I got lost in their beauty. And got myself out of worry and into a can-do mentality. Stop. Look up and look around. There is such beauty in unexpected places.

And for good measure, know that indigenous peoples found that story telling, dancing, singing and silence are universal salves for our souls. I especially recommend the dancing and silence, two things we can never get enough of.

Believing in Wonder Woman's belief

To wrap up and get to the awards, I want to confess that I not only told my healthcare friend that bravery was over-rated. I told her that we shouldn't worship heroes. No one person saves the day. It's about courage and diverse teams of people working together, not heroics.

But then I saw Wonder Woman this weekend and think there may be room for that kind of hero.

At the end of the movie Wonder Woman says to her nemesis:

> *It isn't about what you deserve. It's about what you believe. And I believe in love. Only love will save the world.*

Here's to courage and resiliency and a whole lot of love. And most of all, here's to all of you here today. You are true wonder women and men.

Perseverance Loves to Party

After 2.5 hours of an intense 5Rhythms dance training I was about to literally collapse. The music started to slow, and I thought, "Finally, we're winding down." But no.

Our wonderful teacher Heeraa paused the music and told us that in our exhaustion we would dance our best dances. Our judgmental heads were too tired to interfere with how our bodies really wanted to move.

She might have even said something about being too tired to give a shit how we danced. But I may have been hallucinating.

I do clearly remember that she assured us that our best insights come from listening to what our bodies tell us.

Then she cranked up the trance music.

My bossy pants head said, "Stop now, you don't have to keep up with people 30 or 40 years younger."

My body said, "C'mon girlfriend, stop playing that age excuse card. Let's fly around the dance floor. Perseverance loves to party."

A weird way to up my tenacity

I think I kept going until the end.

That night I felt exhausted and content, kind of peaceful, and maybe numb because not a bone in my 63-year-old body was complaining.

There's a lot of wisdom from conscious dance practices.

But this weekend I reflected on perseverance, especially as it's one of my weakest character traits, like a lot of Rebels at Work.

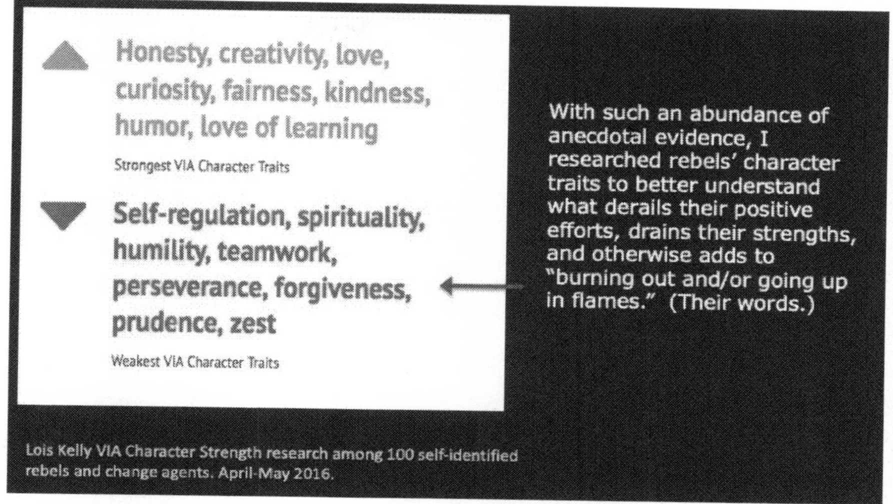

Honesty, creativity, love, curiosity, fairness, kindness, humor, love of learning
Strongest VIA Character Traits
Self-regulation, spirituality, humility, teamwork, perseverance, forgiveness, prudence, zest
Weakest VIA Character Traits
With such an abundance of anecdotal evidence, I researched rebels' character traits to better understand what derails their positive efforts, drains their strengths, and otherwise adds to "burning out and/or going up in flames." (Their words.)
Lois Kelly VIA Character Strength research among 100 self-identified rebels and change agents. April-May 2016.

When we persevere, too exhausted for our brains to get all emotionally wound up in situations at work, we often see things and people in new ways. It's like those aha moments while we're dozing off to sleep. We're not thinking anymore and all of a sudden, a brilliant idea pops.

Or as we're persevering new people join us. If we care that much to keep going, the least that they can do is help get us/our projects to the finish line. As my body moved on the dance floor it picked up energy from everyone else. One guy even took me in his arms, and we did a quick little waltz to the drumbeat of trance music. He gave me new energy.

Most of all, I was reminded that if we practice, we can get better, even at things that we're not innately good at, which for me is perseverance.

And the payoff of tenacity?

I'm sure there are many. Playing the long game to finish difficult challenges can be especially fulfilling and meaningful.

But for me it was something quite simple and luxurious: my body rewarded me with the soundest sleep I've had in years.

ADAPTING AND BOUNCING BACK

Build These Three Change Muscles

Five years ago when people asked me how change happens in big organizations I couldn't wait to share ideas on positioning, navigating organizational politics and conflict.

Now my advice is different.

Based on personal experiences and learning from successful Rebels at Work, Change Agents, social scientists and psychologists, I see the importance of appreciation, character strengths and safety. These have to come before the tactical strategies and skills.

When we practice these three things we build up our ability to adapt to change and increase the self-esteem needed to initiate change. Plus they're contagious, infecting work mates in the best possible ways.

When I was first introduced to these practices I was skeptical, believing them "soft." But almost a year into incorporating them into my life and work I'm singing that 1960s Monkees song, "I'm a Believer." As are many of my clients who are using them to change how they work.

Not changing work like using Yammer, but changing how we work with people, appreciating strengths and trying new things, questioning the status quo, and wondering out loud about possibilities without being criticized for not thinking things through. (I was criticized about the latter during many a performance review early in my career.)

Appreciation: the greatest motivator

A sense of appreciation is single most sustainable motivator at work, according to Dr. Adam Grant, author of Give and Take and the Originals.

BUT we are less likely to express gratitude at work than any other place in their lives, according to research by the John Templeton Foundation

That's right. After thanking the Starbucks barista for such an amazing latte, we walk into work grumpy and never think to thank a co-worker for some small thing that they've done especially well.

But here's the deal: when we feel appreciated we become more trusting of others, our self-confidence increases and we're more likely to help others. Plus we're more open to new ideas.

So stop reading right here.

Think of someone at work who you especially value. What are three things they do that make a difference to your group? Write them down quick. OK, now share those things with that person. Wait until you see how much that person lights up. You'll both feel good.

Another research finding: 88% feel better after giving kudos to co-workers.

Character science: what motivates YOU? Your team?

We all have 24 universal character strengths in various degrees, according to extensive research by psychology professors Christopher Peterson and Martin Seligman. These are intrinsic strengths that give us energy. When we're in "the flow" we're probably using our top strengths.

It's helpful to know what your top strengths are and value and use them because they build your self-esteem, creativity and confidence, all necessary to adapt to change at work. (You can take a free assessment at the VIA Character Institute.)

As helpful is to understand the character strengths of your co-workers. When we understand what different people bring to the organization and how they work they way do within a context of character science, we're able to appreciate them in new ways. (There's the connection back to appreciation.)

My top character strengths are honesty and bravery. So rather than seeing my frankness as a "fault"—or as a royal pain in the ass— colleagues can see how it brings value to our work together.

Guiding teams through this process is some of the most exciting work I've done in my career. It opens people up to people—and themselves—in new ways, creating a more positive, open-minded, can-do environment. And who doesn't want more of that at work?

And the research to back up the benefits? According the VIA Institute on Character:

> *71% of employees who believe their managers can name their strengths feel engaged and energized by their work.*
>
> *For organizations that are focused on strengths, 77% of their employees report they are flourishing, engaged and able to make things happen at work.*

(Aside: this is what employee engagement is about. Not surveys or p.r. campaigns, but being recognized for who we are and appreciated for how we contribute based on our unique—aka genuine—strengths.)

Psychological safety: the secret to high-performing teams

If the environment doesn't feel safe at work, you're kind of, well, screwed because no one wants to make a wrong move, suggest an idea for which they'll be laughed at, or call out a problem.

If you start practicing appreciation and focus on strengths it will become safer, but creating a safe organizational environment requires much more.

Psychological safety is as important as physical safety at work, but it is largely overlooked and few managers are rewarded for creating this climate of belonging and feeling comfortable.

Check out the excellent New York Times Magazine article, "What Google Learned from Its Quest to Build the Perfect Team" by the journalist Charles

Duhigg.

The most important characteristic of the highest-performing teams at Google? Safety.

You get what you give

One of my favorite songs is "You Get What You Give" by the New Radicals. It's an upbeat song with a dark undercurrent about the challenges of our fast changing, crazy world.

> *This whole damn world can fall apart*
> *You'll be OK, follow your heart*
> *You're in harm's way, I'm right behind.*

Life and work *is* life—evolving, spinning, changing. We can't separate the two. We can't ever, despite the politicians' promises, go back to what was.

What we can do is strengthen our resiliency and ability to adapt. Helping one another show up as ourselves, using the strengths that make us each uniquely us, and appreciating what we *are* accomplishing.

Imagine if more of us felt that if we were in harm's way someone would be right behind us?

You get what you give.

Grief and Growth at Work

All change involves loss and some degree of grief, but we rarely help people—or ourselves —process loss at work. Never mind learn ways to recover and become stronger.

Losing a job. Losing work mates from downsizing. Losing the respect of executives because we challenged their beliefs—beliefs that we know will soon cause problems. Losing the confidence in our employer because they sacrificed beloved organizational values to gain another two percent growth.

We deny our sadness and say things like, "It's just a job, not brain cancer."

We suffer. Beat ourselves up. Become bitter. Curse our bosses and the rigid, hierarchical bureaucracies posing as progressive organizations. We get riled up and think, "Somebody should sue the bastards, for God's sake."

Or we can choose to find meaning and learn from what happened, which not only eases suffering, but can potentially transform our careers.

Post traumatic growth

Admiral Jim Stockdale was repeatedly tortured for eight years as a prisoner of war during the Vietnam War. He didn't have much reason to believe he'd ever make it home. He said he survived by framing the experience as something that would define the rest of his life.

Rather than denying reality or taking on a victim mindset, Admiral Stockdale lived each day in prison trying to help the morale of his fellow prisoners. The overly-optimistic POWs without this mindset, however, didn't fare so well.

Stockdale came out of the war experiencing post-traumatic growth, which is a positive psychological change resulting from adversity. (As opposed to the more commonly known syndrome of post-traumatic stress disorder.)

People who experience post-traumatic growth find a new appreciation for life, new perspectives on work paths, and a renewed sense of meaning.

In fact, some psychological research shows that finding benefits from a trauma can lead to personal transformation, according to University of California/Riverside professor Dr. Sonja Lyubomirsky, author of *The How of Happiness*.

"Focusing on the lessons you can learn from the ordeal will help soften its blow," says Lyubomirsky. "The lessons those realities impart could be patience, perseverance, loyalty or courage. Or perhaps you're learning open-mindedness, forgiveness, generosity or self-control. Research shows that with post-traumatic growth you not only can you survive and recover, you can flourish."

Social support, meaning and self-compassion

Three proven practices to experience post traumatic growth are social support, finding meaning, and self-compassion.

Carmen and I have always said that having a trusted tribe of friends is essential for all who identify as Rebels at Work. While your Rebel Alliance can help make your ideas better and move them through the bureaucracy, these friends can also help you recover from setbacks.

> *"Social support is pretty incredible, a strategy of almost magical proportions," says Dr. Lyubomirsky. "Talking to others about a traumatic experience helps you cope and see the event with a new perspective."*

A second strategy for coping is to find meaning and new perspectives by writing about the experience.

Expressive writing forces us to organize our jumble of thoughts and feelings and construct a new narrative. Dr. James Pennebaker of the University of Texas, who has been studying the benefits of writing for 30 years, found that it is a far more powerful tool for healing than anyone had imagined.

Writing for just 15 minutes a day for four consecutive days can produce lasting results in health, happiness and outlook. His recommended approach and writing prompts can be found here.

The trick, he says, is to not keep writing about the negative incident in the same way.

> *"If you catch yourself telling the same story over and over to get past your distress, rethink your strategy. Try writing or talking about your trauma in a completely different way," Dr. Pennebaker advises in* The Secret Life of Pronouns. *"How would a more detached narrator describe what happened? What other ways of explaining the event might exist?"*

The third strategy is self-compassion, accepting that you're human, acknowledging failures and frustrations and not dwelling on mistakes.

> *"Rather than relentlessly condemning ourselves when we fall, even if our fall is a spectacular one, we do have another option," says Dr. Kristin Neff, author of Self-Compassion: The Proven Power of Being Kind to Yourself.*
>
> *"We can recognize that everyone has times when they blow it, and treat ourselves kindly. Maybe we weren't able to put our best foot forward, but we tried, and falling flat on one's face is an inevitable part of life. An honorable part, in fact."*

If we're really pushing the envelope to do great work, we will fall.

Friends, self-compassion and finding meaning from what happened can help us rise up and push even further.

Hey, Hey: When Nothing Goes as Planned

Nothing is going as planned during this two-day tourist jaunt in Sweden. So many weeks of planning and expectations gone kaput.

Taking the ferry to the archipelago didn't happen yesterday because of heavy rain and wind so I decided I would go see the opera Madame Butterfly at the Opera House. Sold out. OK, then, I'll go to the one-star Michelin restaurant. No reservations. Plan C is the Konserthuset. Nope. The concert tonight is for a private audience.

Instead I board Tram 6 as instructed by the club's web site to get to an edgy part of town to see two progressive rock bands, both fronted by young Swedish women.

As the tram moves out of the inner city I carefully watch the digital screen in the tram for my stop. After people get on at each stop they shake rain off their jackets, close their umbrellas, and open the protective plastic on their baby carriages, smiling at their children.

The tram is no longer in the city. The skin shades of my fellow tram travelers range from milky white to deep ebony. People are wearing headscarves, nose rings, headphones, floral wreaths, Afros, beards and orange lipstick.

OK, Milady?

A young woman whose hair is matted to her head from the rain gets on with a baby carriage and a beagle and parks them by my side. "OK, Milady?" she asks me.

Tram 6 stops again but not at my stop. A young Somalian man tells me that this is the end of the line. It's dark and there are no lights at the tram stop. "Where is this stop," I ask him opening my tourist map and pointing to where I'm trying to get to. He can't help because he doesn't speak English. I have to get off. I am lost.

The young mother with the baby carriage and sad-eyed beagle comes to Milady's rescue, telling me which tram to take and advising me that it will be a 30-minute ride. If I'm on Tram 11 longer than that, I will have missed my stop.

Thirty minutes later I get off at the right stop and walk into a magical concert space.

The woman at the door greets me by saying "Hey, Hey" in that lilting, welcoming Swedish way. It's like having a laid-back cheerleader giving you a personal rah when you walk into a Swedish restaurant or shop. I wanted to say back, "Hey, Hey," I made it. But the young woman is already puzzled to see a woman my age at the club's door. No need to make her think I'm totally nuts.

The venue has worn hardwood floors, sophisticated lighting and sound systems, local beers at the two makeshift bars, and people arm in arm, talking, laughing, kissing as they wait for the show to start.

Shaken awake

My boots are still wet from waiting for Tram 11 and I am out of my familiar environments. I am shaken awake. Observant. Enjoying the right now. So happy my traditional tourist choices didn't pan out.

It's still raining the next day so I do another Plan D and go to the Gothenburg Art Museum. As I walk into the first gallery the painting I see is the original of a postcard I've carried around for years. It reminds me of falling in love with my husband. Here it is, a huge canvas, more beautiful than I imagined.

A statue of a green Norwegian imp with flowers growing out of her head is sitting on a table in the same room. I don't see the connection between the statue and the other art in the room. The security guard explains there is no connection. Someone at the museum just thought the table would look better with something on it.

Nothing has gone as planned and everything is better than planned

The painting reminds me of love and how little time I may have left with my husband.

The music club reminds me of how art happens – welcoming, gritty and unfinished.

And the tram ride with Milady's rescuer and the refugees Sweden has welcomed into its country is like an injection of kindness and compassion.

These reminders of art, love and kindness are my Swedish souvenirs. Unexpected and treasured.

Here's to staying open when our carefully developed plans go awry.

Hey, Hey.

Alone and Not Alone

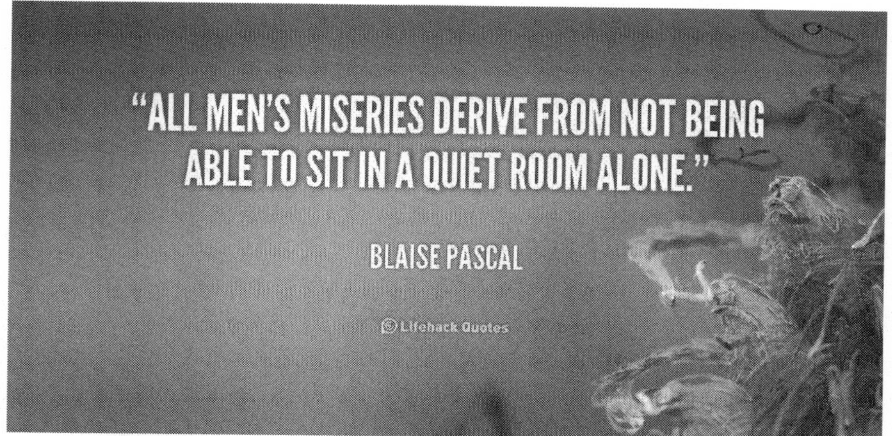

"ALL MEN'S MISERIES DERIVE FROM NOT BEING ABLE TO SIT IN A QUIET ROOM ALONE."
BLAISE PASCAL
Lifehack Quotes

I just got back from a 5-day creative writing retreat with 10 brave, talented artists. It was an intense, exhausting and exhilarating experience where our extraordinary teacher Ann Randolph gently yet firmly pushed us way outside our comfort zones.

We wrote alone, sitting in the same room. And then we read our stories aloud to one another.

It felt sacred, being alone and together. Having time to go deep into our own writing and reflection, and then being able to speak our truths among such a safe, caring group of people.

What does this have to do with being a Rebel at Work? I "re-entered" the work world wondering:

Why are so many work relationships and "team building" attempts so superficial? If there were more ways to share more of the real us, there could be so much more empathy, compassion and psychological safety at work. And with that, more people might speak up and more might listen. And more of the right things might get done faster.

Why don't more people take time to journal about their work to more clearly understand what's happening and put it into perspective? Research shows that when we slow things down and reflect, we're able to be more creative about solving especially challenging problems. Check out this recent HBR post by former CEO Dan Ciampa, "The More Senior Your Job Title, the More You Need to Keep a Journal." (Then insert, "The More Rebellious You Are...")

Similarly, why don't more people take time to think? Especially with close friends. One of the articles I re-read every summer is "Of Solitude and Leadership" by former Yale professor William Dersiewicz, based on his speech to plebes at West Point. It's long, but his perspectives on bureaucracy, complacency and conformity speak to us Rebels. His view on how to "find the strength to challenge an unwise order or wrongheaded policy" is especially wise. And something we can all do.

Why don't more people do the right thing just because it's the right thing? Some of my best writing will never be published. Some of our bravest rebel recommendations will never get us a promotion. But that doesn't mean we shouldn't persevere. Let's stop aiming for the biggest platform to change the world or a bazillion Twitter followers and just do work that matters, however "small" it may seem. Charles' Einstein's recent piece, "The Age of We Need Each Other" captures this thought brilliantly.

I hope you find some time this summer to reflect, have leisurely conversations with friends about ideas that matter, and keep on. You have more talents and innate wisdom than you probably realize.

BE TRUE TO YOURSELF

The Rebel Muhammad Ali

Muhammad Ali's conscientious objection to the War in Vietnam is the first social/political issue I can remember capturing my attention. When Ali refused induction into the military in 1967 I was 12 years old. My family had just returned the previous year from Germany where my dad the Army sergeant had been assigned. We had had no television to speak of in the small Bavarian town of Bad Kissingen, so the ferment of the civil rights movement, for example, didn't penetrate my consciousness. (I remember when we landed in the United States from Germany being transfixed by an American television show—a black and white episode of *Lost in Space* featuring Billy Mumy—broadcast somewhere in the airport.)

Everything about the Muhammad Ali case confused me.

Of course most people then were still calling him Cassius Clay, including my parents. My father had no sympathy for Ali's refusal to go to Vietnam and yet he had admired the brash irreverence of Cassius Clay the boxer. I remember wondering why such an attractive person would risk all that success by making an unpopular argument. I couldn't imagine anything ever being so important.

And yet I also remember disagreeing with Ali's critics who questioned his patriotism and manhood. The one thing he didn't seem to lack was courage.

Fifty years later, Carmen the adult-approaching-senior-citizen has achieved more clarity about the example of Muhammad Ali. In a wonderful retrospective I recommend to all Rebels at Work, Ali is quoted as saying during the height of the controversy:

I have nothing to lose by standing up for my beliefs.

Actually, he had just about everything to lose materially. Because of his decision, Ali was stripped of his heavyweight boxing title—the most prestigious athletic honor of that era—and was unable to fight during what should have been his most productive years. He lost a lot.

But, as the article makes clear, Ali's principled stand buttressed others to do what they thought was right, including female tennis star Billie Jean King and Nelson Mandela, who, it should be remembered, was a heavyweight boxer himself in 1950s South Africa.

I think Muhammad Ali intuited the impact that a single individual can have when he stands for something beyond just himself. He took on the most extreme of positions at the most inopportune of times and was ready to suffer the consequences if proven wrong. He understood what a 12-year old couldn't and what many adults still don't:

Life's ultimate success is being true to yourself.

Bring Your Soul to Work

The malaise of work is a spiritual crisis.

Not spiritual in the religious sense. But spiritual in our yearning to have more joy, kindness, respect and compassion at work. Spiritual in our desire to grow our capacity to learn, help, care, imagine, forgive, and support others – and they us — when we push ourselves into the scary territory of doing new types of work. Spiritual in that we want to be devoted to our work, but not slaves to it.

To change corporate cultures is almost impossible. But perhaps what we can do is bring our best selves to work, allowing our spiritual longings to run free, and in doing so, infect others.

By our best selves I mean doing work that matters to us. That we, for some reason, are truly good at. So good, in fact, you could say we become devoted to our work.

I don't mean devoted to our company's purpose. The reality is that most organizations don't have an inspirational purpose that stirs our heart and soul. They're about serving customers, making money, and hopefully, providing decent wages and an ethical work environment. You can search a whole lifetime to find an organization with a "meaningful purpose" and come up empty. Or you can find one with an inspiring purpose and walk into a cold, cynical culture.

> *Rather than focus on company purpose, perhaps we should focus on personal devotion. By devotion I mean what you care about and find satisfaction in being able to do well.*

A friend who works for a global transportation company felt trapped in a job that left him spiritually bereft.

"I just don't feel like this company is changing the world in any meaningful way. I need more purpose at work. Some days I wish I could just paint more," he said.

"You're an artist!" I asked. Who knew.

Over dinner he told me how creativity is so important to him, and then we started exploring how he could bring more creativity to his work inside a big company. How he might be able to devote himself to developing creative product and service solutions. How maybe he could devote himself to creativity at work, period.

He's now head of innovation and design and happier and more energized than I've seen him in the past 10 years. His spirit is infectious, too.

The wonderful thing about being devoted to *your* work and finding meaning from it. is that your humanity – kindness, caring, compassion – grows and affects others at work, at home and with friends.

The frame of your devotion can also help you envision where to take your work, reaching beyond companies, functions and specialties.

What are you devoted to?

I've always been devoted to helping people, causes and companies be understood. This has taken me from working in marketing positions, advising industry leaders, serving on non-profit boards, coaching sales executives on big pitches, and volunteering on community issues. The devotion is the same. The application is different. The meaning is always there.

One of my brothers owns a sand and gravel company. For years I thought he was devoted to making big buckets of money. But I have come to appreciate how devoted he is to helping his largely uneducated, immigrant employees live the American dream. He works so much because his work is a spiritual — though he would never probably be comfortable in talking about it in this way.

With the publication of Rebels at Work: A Handbook for Leading Change from Within, many people have asked me why I got involved in this topic. Rebels? Really?

Helping people in big organizations have their often-provocative ideas be understood fits my devotion.

Spiritual prophets at work?

The other reason is that people devoted enough to speak up for important and unpopular ideas may be the spiritual prophets at our workplaces. They bring courage, creativity, commitment and a belief that there's always a way to improve work, making things better for people..

It's hard to change the world or even our companies. But maybe, just maybe we can make work more spiritual by bringing our best selves to our work and positively affecting others.

The Latin meaning of devotion is vow.

What might happen if more of us vowed to do work that brings us alive?

The World Is Fast: an Ode to Daring Work

The world is fast.

Fads.

Technology.

Terrorism.

Viral diseases.

Natural disasters.

Pop-up stores.

Food trucks.

Trending tweets.

Viral videos.

Bull markets.

Bear markets.

Sudden death.

Market crashes

Medical miracles.

ADHD.

Random collisions.

Unexpected introductions.

The three a.m. eureka.

We are slow.

Resisting.

Doubting.

Looking for proof.

Seeking certainty.
Denying our yearnings.
Discrediting our hunches.
Waiting for someone else.
Hoping for a hero.
Worrying about mistakes.
Seeing things through a warped lens.
Remembering before.
Longing for the predictable.

Take one step.
Then another.
Skip.
Jump.
Run.
Twirl.
Let go.
Dive in.

Feel the energy.
The wind helping you go faster.
The unusual friendships.
The laughter from the unexpected.
The surprise that you are safe.
The surprise that work is different.
The relief that you are relevant. Running rather than being dragged.

The world is fast and furiously asking us to take our feet off the brakes.
We are all skidding.
Take your foot off the brake.
Steer into your work.
Into your life.
Into the world.

VI

Leading Rebels

Section Highlights: Leading Rebels

We like to say that *Rebels at Work* is a rarity among business books—written not for the CEO or senior manager but for the average working man or woman. And yet over the years we've written many blog posts offering ideas for managers who want to take full advantage of the Rebel brilliance in their work force.

The truth is that many leaders want to hear from their staffs and are open to new ways of doing work, but don't quite know how to start the dialogue. And the average employee, perhaps already burned by speaking up "inappropriately," needs a lot of convincing to abandon her "the boss is always right" approach.

We became famous for our bad rebel, good rebel chart, and we've recently developed a similar treatment for the Status Quo. Just like rebels, who are often viewed as troublemakers, the Status Quo can have a bad side and a good side.

Study the chart for some adjustments leaders can make to change the dynamic of their organization and invite more Rebel input.

Bad Status Quo	Good Status Quo
Demands	Inquires
Enforces Rules	Refreshes Rules
Stability-focused	Mission-focused
Avoids Problems	Discovers opportunities
Invites	Includes
Consolidates	Distributes
Prescribes	Experiments
Determines	Learns
Worries	Anticipates
Defines	Explores

Several other blog posts provide more general advice for leaders who want to be effective managers of rebels. And the Tao of Rebel Management is directed at managers and leaders who themselves are serving as Rebels in their organization.

What has become quite clear in the last ten years is that promoting Diversity of Thought in organizations helps their bottom line. One of the best ways for leaders to make space for Rebels at Work is to create a work environment that is open to all ideas. We share best practices for promoting Diversity of Thought, including a counterintuitive lesson from me (Carmen) that managers benefit from being a bit lazy.

Although not always made explicit, organizations and their leaders value smooth operations and seek to avoid messiness and uncertainty. Unfortunately, innovation and the implementation of new ideas tend to create disruption. We offer numerous suggestions for leaders to avoid stability traps.

Good relations between leaders and team members depend upon emotional intelligence skills. Lois shares what being a parent has taught her about being a Rebel Boss.

MANAGERS: DO MORE OF THIS

Useful Tactics for Rebel Managers

During my government career, I had probably about a five-year period when I was in positions that offered me broad influence within my Agency. During this time I thought hard about how to gain support for the ideas I cared about, but thinking hard, while essential, is not sufficient to make change happen. Doing hard is better. Reflecting back on that time, I can't help but think that I ~~squandered~~ didn't optimize the opportunity. Which means that many of the tactics I share here are the insights of hindsight.

These first two are most important.

Before you do anything else, master the bureaucratic landscape

This could just about kill most rebels, I think, because I have met few who are bureaucratic natives. **But rest assured, the defenders of THAT WHICH REFUSES TO BUDGE** are bureaucratic black belts. They know every trick in the book of regulations that—like mortar—holds the status quo together.

My advice: before you announce your great vision, before you share your ideas with others, spend as much time as you can developing an understanding of how the bureaucracy works and of all the ways previous reform efforts failed—and believe me there have been previous ones. (Six months for this pre-work sounds about right to me.)

Perhaps you can find a lawyer in your organization or one of those individuals who are professional chiefs of staff and executive officers: you know these people, the ones who may not know the substance of making better widgets but they know every process and admin trick to get things done. Spend some time with them anticipating who will fight your efforts and what venues and tactics they will use. The military has a great term for this: preparing the battlefield. In short, anticipate everything. Anticipation is the essential lubricant of good management.

The second equally important and quite related tactic.

Sequence, sequence, sequence

As a rebel, achieving a position of influence in an organization is rare. You will almost certainly not get an opportunity to reboot or do over. Therefore the order in which you tackle things is key.

After you prepare the bureaucratic field for battle, then you need to think through the optimum order for the actions you will take. There is no school solution to how one should sequence, methinks, because local conditions vary. But take the time to think it through. Are there some people you need to get on your side before you make the big launch? When is the optimum time to make a play for money in your organization? Should you start your reforms in one part of the organization first and then seek to grow from there? Or will that only give the enemies of change more time to organize their defenses?

Start small, unless you think it best to start big!

OK, I know, that's a total cop-out. But my guess is that more often than not, but definitely not always, starting small is not a bad innovation strategy. I wrote about the principles of disruptive innovation in government in a Deloitte Perspectives post recently. Disruptive innovators, according to Clayton Christensen, 1) serve underserved customers or markets with 2) new technologies that initially provide a lesser product or service but 3) are less expensive than their competitors.

Now let's say you've got your reform Radio Flyer rolling along. (That's actually a term I used once to describe a change effort I was spearheading. I used it to make the point that I wanted to be able to carry everything people needed to know about the new widgets and processes we were building in a Radio Flyer wagon. It needed to be that simple.)

Now what are some things you can do to ensure your reform effort keeps chugging uphill? (And Comrades, it will be uphill all the way. There is no downhill run when you're in the change business. In fact one way you know you're making headway is when it becomes harder and harder to pull or push. The forces of gravity grow just as you're about to crest the hill.)

Make sure your calendar reflects your priorities

If you're in a position of authority and you're talking about the need for change, all the other bureaucrats will be watching your actions carefully to be sure you mean what you say. Even those who want to support you will not want to identify themselves prematurely.

So be sure the meetings you attend and the people you have time for are consistent with your stated priorities. This hearkens to one of the points I've previously made: don't let the status quo capture you with their battle rhythm. Spend your time doing what you say is important.

For example, one of the ways diversity initiatives can fail in organizations is if the only time the issue is discussed is at the once-a-year diversity meeting. If diversity is important to you, then it should permeate everything you do and be discussed **ALL THE TIME**.

Speaking of meetings, one of the things I learned too late is that:

Conflict-free meetings should rarely be your goal

If what you're doing is important, people should be objecting and arguing with you. The way ahead often has poor signage. But too often in bureaucracies, we're taught that conflict in meetings is bad and we should seek consensus. Remember:

Consensus is just a way to Avoid Making Decisions

Consensus is not a decision-making strategy. In fact it is the opposite. It's a technique to avoid making difficult choices.

And my last piece of tactical advice is actually a riddle.

What do the organizational rebel and the NFL running back have in common?

Cue music....

They both need to hit their holes quickly.

React like a running back!

Just as in football, bureaucratic holes open and close quickly. If you've thought through and sequenced your strategy, you'll be more likely to recognize a bureaucratic opening when it happens. When you spot it, don't dawdle. Run through it as quickly as you can.

If you're lucky and good, you'll score!

When You Manage Rebels: a Long Overdue Blog Post

I promised I would share my lessons on how to be a manager of rebels more than two months ago, which just goes to show you how fast time flies....**PERIOD**. Time's a wastin', so let's get started.

Here's the scenario: you have somehow reached a position of authority and some flexibility in your organization. You have some kind of bully pulpit and control of some resources, and you find yourself drawn to some kind of change agenda.

Perhaps you, like I at my previous employer, were a rebel when you were just a worker bee and you would like to encourage and support the colleagues you know who are rebels and change agents too. Or maybe you have never described yourself as a rebel but now that you're in higher management you believe it's time to encourage some new energy and new ideas in your organization. What should you do? What shouldn't you do?

(Methodology note: these comments are based on my personal experiences, what I've observed in almost 35 years in the work place, and the many conversations I've been having with others who know more.)

What to do

Find a way to meet regularly with random people throughout the organization. This may seem unrelated and a strange place to start, but my reasoning is this: if you are going to use your time at the top to support rebels, you need to keep informed on what's really going on in the organization. It's absolutely amazing how quickly power isolates you: my sense is that you become compromised within six weeks of assuming a senior position.

My approach at the Agency was to try to have dinner with random groups of analysts at least every other month. When I say random, I mean random. I would somehow run into someone who worked for me (once I ran into a fellow at one of the rest stops on I-95 for example.) I would ask the person to gather a group of people he or she knew; I nor anyone else would vet the names. And we would have dinner.

There were just a couple of rules. You could not be critical of a person, although you could be critical of a position or type of person, like branch chiefs. And we at some point had to talk about something other than work. That was it.

I probably had dinner with close to 100 analysts in two years. The amplification effects of these conversations were incredible.

Another "trick" I used was reaching out to everyone on Instant Messaging on their birthday. (I actually had HR run a list of the entire workforce by date of birth (but not the year to stay clear of any equity or discrimination issues, although I did get to figure out everyone's horoscope sign that way.) This activity, which maybe took ten minutes on an average day, turned out to be an absolutely fascinating psychological experiment. Some individuals were embarrassed and/or couldn't wait to end the conversation; others engaged me in small talk; and a very small group—I suspect all rebels or rebel aspirants—engaged me immediately in a conversation about some aspect of how work was done. My rule was that if the issue required more time than we had then, they would get a followup meeting.

Give Rebels real work to do. Once the organization identifies you as a rebel (and let's be truthful, most smart leadership teams cultivate one or two "house rebels"), then they'll start assigning you to these special rebel tasks.

I can't tell you how many different task forces and working groups I served on during my Agency career on some aspect of Change and the Agency. While the first one or two of these assignments was interesting, they soon became moderately depressing.

Being asked to do "rebel work" is also a career killer. Most rebels are already distraught at having to choose between speaking their mind and stoking their career. Rebels often hear in performance appraisal sessions how while their work on such-and-such change initiative was admirable, it did distract them from the mission. Don't make this phenomenon worse by heaping more such assignments on them. So what's an example of real work?

Bring your rebels into key support positions in your organization. Make them your Chief of Staff, for example. Encourage others on the Executive Team to do the same. Every organization has key positions that lubricate all the other processes. Executive Office, Chief of Staff, many other names. These are usually filled by classic high-performing, hard chargers.

Try a different approach. Bring someone who is known for having different ideas into these positions. The benefits and down-the-road payoffs will be huge, I guarantee. The rebels will learn to be much more realistic and effective in their approach to change. The executive team will benefit from a more nuanced and forward-looking perspective.

Do something concrete in support of your rebels. If you're at the top of an organization, saying that you support change or an idea espoused by a rebel is significant, but not significant enough. Everyone in the organization will look to see if you intend to support your words with concrete actions.

One clear step is to provide money for implementation, but sometimes, for example in most governments, shifting resources is not that simple, or can only be done at certain times of the year.

When I was at the Agency, I was known as a supporter of Intellipedia. I made a point of speaking at as many of the Intellipedia training sessions as I possibly could. My memory is these were held every other week; my executive assistant knew it was a priority. By showing up at well over half of the sessions and spending an hour talking to each class, I demonstrated my commitment extended beyond pronouncements.

What NOT to do

Mistake bellyachers and troublemakers with rebels. This is a problem that can particularly afflict non-rebel managers. You want to promote change and some change agents, but you're not sure who's the real deal and who's not. I also think it's useful to remember that most "good rebels' are reluctant rebels. The mantle of rebellion does not rest easily on their shoulders. So if you want to know who the real rebels are, keep your ears to the ground and talk to everyone not just the self-appointed change agents.

Assign rebels to the New, High-Profile Center for Innovation. This is a cousin of **Do Give Rebels Real Work to Do** above, so I won't repeat what I said there. But I will add that nothing can be more dispiriting for many rebels than to be asked to lead the organization's new Center for Innovation. As my colleague Lois Kelly discovered in her survey of corporate rebels a couple of years ago, most rebels are at best lukewarm about being asked to serve on special innovation projects. Too many innovation centers pursue change for the sake of change or new for the sake of new. Innovation needs to be centered on and central to the mission.

Force your rebels to behave heroically. Although organizational heroism is a useful tactic, it is not, in my view, the basis of a long-term strategy. What are some ways that a well-meaning manager can unintentionally force a rebel to behave heroically? How about asking her to make a solo presentation to the executive team about a new change initiative? Ouch!! Or asking a rebel to write a critique, just for the manager, of an organization's new strategic plan. Both of these examples resemble realities I have observed. Most serious rebels have survived by mastering the indirect approach. As in the military, asking the rebels to take the point position is like asking them to step voluntarily into the ambush. It's really just a more sophisticated way of throwing your rebels under the bus.

Want to Be a Better Leader? Be a SAP.

First off, I must confess that this blog post is one of those annoyingly not-so-clever ones that attempts to peddle a contrived acronym as a pearl of wisdom. Yup, eventually I'll reveal what SAP actually stands for so that the readers can be amazed.

Perhaps some readers are already amazed that we're writing a blog post about how leaders can improve. "I thought Rebels at Work were decidedly anti-management."

Well, yes, we don't often sing its praises. And that's what actually spurred the writing of this post. We take so many shots at managers that the reader might legitimately wonder "What are managers good for, anyway?" That's a good question for which there are many bad answers out there.

I remember when I had my first management job at the CIA in 1984, I spent two dreadful weeks trying to do what I thought a manager should do. I was rather humorless, uncharacteristically attentive to details, and constantly telling my "subordinates" what to do. Lucky for me and the "underlings," I was also miserable. After two weeks, I decided to behave in ways that made me happy, which had little in common with 1980s management-speak.

One quite popular book then was *In Search of Excellence*. I penned a little ditty about it at the time, sung to the tune of Enjoy Yourself, It's Later than You Think, which I would perform at CIA holiday parties. Luckily no cameras are allowed on the CIA campus.

You work and work for years and years on Uncle Sam's payroll,
Protecting the American way from Communistic foes.

And then one day they tell you that you reek of indolence!
Imagine all the fun we'll have In Search of Excellence.
Away we go, In Search of Excellence
Write a Credo, In Search of Excellence...

But I digress...

So what are managers good for, anyway, I asked myself. What can they uniquely do to make the workplace better that doesn't duplicate others' efforts and/or doesn't somehow depress the energy of motivated employees? The first word that came to mind was:

Anticipation

To my way of thinking, the one talent that managers/leaders must have is the ability to anticipate—to see around the corner to identify the annoying problem or the frisky opportunity.

Other colleagues—even the "underlings"—can anticipate as well, but if the team has a broadish area of responsibility with multiple moving parts, the manager of the unit is the one person in a position to see more connections and thus anticipate what others can't. If a manager/leader doesn't anticipate well, they are failing at their primary, unique contribution.

Anticipation is not the same thing as Vision. You often hear that the leader's job is to set the vision for her team, advice that I find disturbing but that I often see leaders follow. "I'm excited to be presenting my vision to the team tomorrow." Ugh!!

The last thing a leader should do is present a unilateral vision of the way forward to his "subordinates." People do not freely endorse what is imposed upon them. A leader's responsibility is to facilitate well the process through which goals and objectives are agreed to. Everyone on the team has an important role to play here.

Rather than visionary, anticipation is often tactical. It can be as tactical as realizing that too many people will be out of the office at the same time in August. But short-term can be quite important.

For example, there are many contractors serving the Federal Government who now wish they had done a better job of anticipating a government shutdown. And anticipation is more than just suspecting what the next turn of events might be. It is important to appreciate the consequences of that event and what your team's next steps might be.

Selection

The second unique responsibility for managers/leaders is selecting individuals for their team and helping individuals match their talents to the right tasks.

I remember a CIA director once saying to me that the best way to get something done is to put someone in charge of doing it. Now this seems like ridiculously obvious advice although it is still overlooked in large organizations and bureaucracies. But the statement conveys more meaning with the simple addition of one word: "The best way to get something done is to put the ***right*** someone in charge of doing it." Now it becomes clear.

The best form of quality control is hiring the best person for the job. It's that simple and that hard. All other methods of quality control are inferior, tend to waste time, and risk eroding morale. In knowledge work, for example, controlling for quality almost always involves stopping the flow of work to allow the higher authority to weigh in. And "weigh in" is an appropriate metaphor, as the hierarchical intervention almost always comes down like a ton of bricks.

Managers/leaders don't always make optimum hires. But you can always adjust by helping the colleague match their talents to the right tasks. In my experience, the majority of "performance" issues among the "underlings" involves a bad fit. When everyone on a team is well-fitted, the manager's job in terms of quality control, is trivial.

Perspective

The final letter in my acronym is P for Perspective. Merriam Webster's second definition for perspective is "the interrelation in which a subject or its parts are mentally viewed; the capacity to view things in their true relations or relative importance." Just as was the case with anticipation, managers/leaders are in the best position to keep things in perspective. In fact, perspective is a key prerequisite for anticipation.

Managers who lack perspective are bitter disappointments for their "subordinates." The inability to distinguish the truly important from the bureaucratically necessary exhausts everybody. Lack of perspective leads to monotonous meetings and pointless taskings. When we speak of people who have common sense or good intuitions, what we are likely identifying is a keenly developed sense of perspective.

OK, so I've spelled ASP. I wrote about these in the order that I thought of them, but ASP obviously wouldn't do, although no doubt many of you do suspect many leaders are snakes after all. So there you have it, a contrived acronym hoping to convey a modicum of wisdom.

When in Sweden: Leadership Lessons from the Scrum

I spent last week in Malmo speaking at the øredev software developers conference. I was a bit dubious as to how relevant presentations on surviving as a change agent or diversity of thought would be to the assembled coders and programmers. Not only was I wrong about their appetite for learning how to be a more effective rebel at work but, more important, I learned a lot from them about how to manage teams in more effective ways.

At the risk of embarrassing myself with my ignorance about modern approaches to software development, I can report that the developer community appears to be some distance ahead of many other work domains in rethinking how to manage teams.

Much software demands continuous updating. And old styles of project management simply can't handle that speed of flow. Stopping work for quality control purposes is just not tenable in an era of continuous development. (And in any case, such control doesn't actually lead to quality. Chokepoints such as software approval boards, for example, don't actually correlate with more quality.)

Even when I was a manager of analysis at the CIA, it occurred to me that the supposed need for quality control from managers usually stalled the entire sensemaking process. This could get pretty bad when a manager "sat on the product", taking days if not weeks to judge it worthwhile. One of my "rebel" ideas was to wonder if we could ensure quality without a linear editorial process. The software community has made much more progress than I ever did.

Instead of the linear "waterfall" process, which many organizations still employ today, the favored approach to software development is agile, which stresses simultaneous work across many streams. Work is managed more collaboratively within a team using approaches such as Kanban and Scrum. I would just reveal even more of my ignorance if I tried to explain these concepts in any depth, so check out articles such as this one.

The relevance for rebels at work is that agile approaches should make it easier for team members to offer up new and different ideas. That's certainly the hope.

Some of my favorite takeaways from the conference, in no particular order.

Striving for 100% efficiency in utilization of resources just leads to more mistakes. Several presenters made this point, which reminded me of the cult of "busyness" we find in so many organizations. Google for example, expects its staff members to meet 70% of their key objectives. Demanding much more stifles innovation and flexibility. Over-commitment to goals is not healthy.

I was introduced to Brook's Law, which states that adding more people to a late project only makes it later. What a gem! Adding more people just creates more hand-offs, more ignorance, more back-briefing, etc. So many organizations panic and make this mistake.

You can have too much micromanagement, but you can also have too much servant leadership as well. This chart from a presentation by Pete Behrens illustrates the happy medium of management styles.

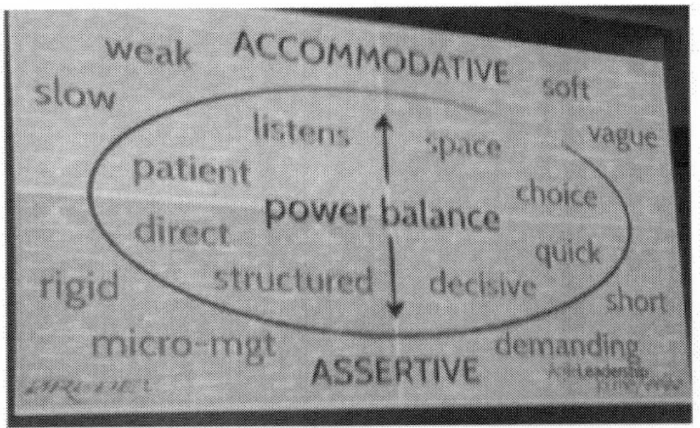

The things people do in an organization tend to get mirrored in its software code. One presenter noted that he can identify healthy or sick organizations just by looking at the software code of their key processes. That was fascinating and I wondered whether in fact sort of the reverse might be true. Can you change organizational culture by adopting new software programs? I wonder.

And my favorite:

The courage to not know nurtures team agility and growth. I think this also came from Pete Behrens' presentation. When team leaders or scrum masters hesitate to answer questions, they provide others on the team the opportunity to teach. Silence can also be an important superpower for rebels at work. Ask yourself if you give your colleagues enough opportunity to contribute their ideas. Or do you always dominate the conversation with your brilliant thoughts?

Here's a handy term to recall when you feel yourself sucking the air out of the room.

W.A.I.T: Why Am I Talking.

The Tao of Rebel Management

Earlier this month I talked about the bearable discomfort of being a rebel, although some who commented didn't find it very bearable. (And we should not minimize reality or sugar it. It can be very painful to be a rebel. Figuring out ways to make it less hard by learning from each other is the purpose of this community.)

Since that post I've been reflecting on my time as a senior leader at the CIA, when I, as a known rebel, was, rather unexpectedly, asked to actually help steer the enterprise. So many mistakes I made!! Some lessons I learned soon enough to be of help at the time; but sadly too many were only apparent in hindsight. I've decided to organize them into three broad categories:

- The Tao of Rebel Management
- Useful Tactics for Rebel Managers
- Helping Rebels Help Themselves

The last category captures the dual challenge confronting rebel managers. On the one hand you are now in a position to actually try to implement some of the ideas you care most deeply about. On the other hand, you also are in a position to help others, most of whom were presumably your colleagues, fellow members of the rebel alliance. You might think it would be easy to do both simultaneously. I did not find that to be the case, but more on that later.

This post focuses on the Tao of Rebel Management. These are broad principles; you could call many of them useful states of mind, to carry with you on your rebel management tour of duty. Many of these ideas I've already catalogued on my RecoveringFed blog under Lessons from a CIA Manager because they are in fact just principles of good leadership. But some are new and almost all have a special rebel wrinkle.

Be corny! I know this advice is personality dependent and some of you may just not be able to go there. But when you embark on your effort to change **THAT WHICH REFUSES TO BUDGE**, act as if success is just around the corner. Be cheerful! Be emotional! Evince some enthusiasm. (Organizations tend to view enthusiasm as some kind of sin—and of course cynics can't abide it.) I can't think of anything less appealing than a dour reformer. (Not to mention that those who oppose you are just waiting for you to lose your cool and your momentum.)

There's actually an important reason to start off positive, because soon enough you will need to accept the fact that you will have to.

Disappoint your followers at a rate they can tolerate. This is not an original thought. Ron Heifetz came up with this concept some ten years ago. Rebel managers soon enough will start making compromises as they work to master the art of possible change in their organization. Almost all of your supporters will be disappointed by the compromises you make but you can't afford to lose their good will completely. Zen rebel managers are particularly skilled at navigating this narrow path.

When you join the management team, you will soon become acquainted with the quaint customs and time-honored procedures of the TOP. Many of these stroke your ego and make you feel important. But you must resist!

Establish your own leadership tempo. It's not just the trappings of power that the rebel manager must avoid. She needs to resist being sucked into the daily, weekly, monthly rhythm of meetings beloved by the status quo. These meetings are powerful defense mechanisms of **THAT WHICH REFUSES TO BUDGE**. If you let these meetings exhaust your time and energy, you're in trouble from the get-go. Don't accept the routines and customs of the existing management team. Question for example why you really must read every single memo produced by the office and whether the "update meetings" really are necessary.

Understand the power of love. Whose love? The love of many in your organization for the way things are, for the status quo. I think this is one of the greatest mistakes rebel managers can make: failing to understand that many, if not most, of the other leaders of their organization want to preserve what they have because they genuinely believe in it. Those who oppose change aren't stupid or acting only out of self-interest. For many, the changes the rebel managers advocate strike at the very essence of something they believe in deeply. Once you understand this, your approach changes. You are less likely to underestimate those who don't support you and much more willing to engage in real conversations with them to identify areas for synergy.

These conversations will prepare you to:

Seek progress, not perfection. Rebel managers often have only a relatively short time to effect change. It is exhausting and difficult to fend off all the tactics that will be deployed against you. So be sure to take all the gains that are offered, however trivial they may seem.

Change your change agenda. Don't stand pat with the same reform ideas you've had for ten years. As a rebel manager, you are being exposed to new information about how the system really works. You can be sure that the ideas you came in determined to implement need adjustment. Some rebel managers will resist doing so lest they appear weak or inconsistent. Don't conflate your ego with your ideas.

Ignore your lizard brain. As you work on your reform program, you will encounter situations that drive you crazy, that make you want to give up. And you'll feel these acid emotions start massing in your brain. These are the emotions that, left unchecked, will lead you to yell at someone, wield sarcasm, and have too many drinks when you get home. Learn to recognize the acid buildup early on. What I've actually found useful, as soon as I sense these primitive emotions, is simply to start saying, preferably out loud, the phrase "lizard brain." It works almost like an exorcism. As soon as I recognize the emotions for what they are, they lose their power.

PROMOTE DIVERSITY OF THOUGHT

Advice for Managers: Do You Make it Easy for People to Disagree with You?

This Friday I was telling a story about an experience I had in a meeting many years ago. I was new to these meetings; I had just been promoted to a new position. A serious decision was being made and as I listened to the discussion it became clear to me that one important aspect of the decision was not going to be discussed. I knew this was not a trivial issue but I also realized it probably fell in the category of "elephant in the room people had probably long decided not to talk about." At the time I weighed two considerations:

I don't think we can make the best decision if we don't discuss this issue. In fact, it is wrong not to discuss it.

As the new person at the table, suspecting what I do about the past care and feeding of elephants, if I mention this at my first meeting I risk being branded as a troublemaker and perhaps even losing my seat at the table.

And so I said nothing. It has always troubled me I said nothing.

As I told this story one insightful young man asked me:

"Could the leader of the meeting have done something to make you feel comfortable enough to ask the question?"

As a leader, particularly during challenging, change-infested times like these, it's your responsibility, your obligation to ensure people feel comfortable in saying what they really think about the decisions you want to make and the opinions you have.

I know this runs counter to the "strong personality as leader" archetype many of us carry around in our heads, but it is nevertheless essential if you want to ensure your organization considers all points of view. (This archetype, by the way, provides a convenient excuse for individuals in the workplace not to be more proactive in offering up their suggestions.)

So what could the leader of the meeting have said or done:

Groups should have a pre-approved checklist of issues to consider every time an important decision is made. Once the checklist is followed, the leader should ask if there are additional issues to consider in this instance.

Groups should imagine how their opponents would view the decision. Would they welcome what we have done? How would they try to take advantage of it.

The leader could ask: **What are we missing?**

The leader could ask: **How could we be wrong in this decision?**

The leader could ask: **If we find out a week from now the decision was wrong, what would have been the cause?**

I'm not, by the way, fond of the idea of the leader turning to the new person in the room and asking them what they think. That puts them in the hot seat in precisely the way they want to avoid.

Millennials at Work

"I'll never have as many new ideas as I do now, and yet no one wants to listen to me."

"What really bothers me is the lack of honesty. When they interviewed me they said they were interested in my creativity and new ideas, and yet now that I'm on the job, I realize that if I challenge the way things are done, I'll just get slapped."

"I really want to help the government do better, but I'm afraid of getting trapped in a bureaucracy."

"He told me to be quiet and wait my turn. And in 20 years I'd be in a position to change things. And so I left."

This is how many Millennials describe to us their experiences and fears about today's workplace. They care about making a difference, but just aren't prepared to sacrifice their souls in the process. They've heard all the talk about how they have unrealistic expectations and should just wait their turn and pay their dues. But what should they do, they ask us, if they think they have good ideas right now? Why doesn't the organization want to take advantage of new ideas and fresh thinking during such times of disruptive innovation?

Why indeed! Although Lois and I are decades past our entry points into the workforce, we both recall acutely how it felt when we first realized that the organizations we worked for weren't necessarily interested in our best ideas. Some of our best ideas were horrible or naïve or both, but a few of them weren't so bad really.

The cost for organizations of ignoring the ideas of your new hires seems much higher today.

When I started work in 1978, the technology in my office hadn't changed in 20 years, maybe not even since World War II. I wrote on an old typewriter that had been around for years. I used a land line. And a ball point, although if you were really cool you insisted on a fountain pen.

Today, however, Millennials bring into most work places a native familiarity with new ways of thinking and doing that organizations say they really want and need. It really doesn't even make sense to ask them to wait five years for their voices to matter, let alone 20.

You can even make the case that if organizations really want to boost their creativity and innovation, they should go out of their way to harvest the ideas of their younger, newer employees. After all, young men and women in their 20s have given birth to some of the most convention-shattering ideas in human history.

- Einstein was 26 when he published his paper on the theory of relativity.
- Isaac Newton postulated the theory of gravity when he was 23.
- The founding generation of the United States was famously young. On 4 July 1776, Betsy Ross was 24, Nathan Hale 21, James Madison 25, and Tom Jefferson was 33. (Ben Franklin of course was 70!)
- A 27-year old Coco Chanel opened her first boutique in France.
- JK Rowling got the idea for Harry Potter at the age of 25.
- By the time he was 25, Mark Zuckerburg had been running Facebook for five years.
- And it was a 29 year-old Elon Musk who founded the company that would eventually become Paypal.

These individuals either worked outside organizations or founded them. I suspect, in fact, that a correlation exists between the growth and importance of organizations in the last 100 years and the popularity of concepts such as paying your dues and biding your time.

So while we have a tendency to write about individuals who have been struggling for many years to make organizational change happen, it's time to acknowledge that you can find yourself a Rebel at Work within the first few weeks of your first job. Those "wiser and older" will tell Millennials to just cool it. But the better option for the smart organization may be to ask Millennials to "bring it on."

Ask More Questions and Tell Fewer Lies

Lois and I made a conscious decision to write *Rebels at Work* for fellow rebels lacking leadership positions in large organizations. There were at least two other audiences we could have written for:

The Rebel Manager. Someone actually in a leadership position trying to take an organization in a different direction. That's whom I usually think of when I hear the term Change Agent.

The Manager of Rebels. Here we're referring to "bosses" who want to be helpful to their "rebels." Often they recognize the need for innovation, but don't have the ideas themselves. Or don't want to be the front person for a change initiative but wouldn't mind supporting people willing to take the lead.

I think sometimes Rebels at Work can be overly critical of managers who recognize a problem but don't want to push the solution directly. Sure, some of them are playing it overly safe, but others may have good reasons to demur. They may have fought many battles earlier in their careers, and just don't have enough juice left for another push. Or they realize they may not have enough influence in their hierarchy to pursue a direct approach.

These well-intended managers of rebels keep asking us some great questions at talks we've given recently. And a lot of them revolve around how to manage a team of individuals holding strong opinions. You would think managers would want teams of strong thinkers. HA! We all know managers are still trained and many are in any case inclined to achieve homogeneity and harmony in the work place What is otherwise lovingly referred to as CONSENSUS.

Luke Visconti of Diversity Inc. wrote in his Ask the White Guy column:

> *The dominant culture, regardless of who it is or where it is, is driven to value conformity.*

If more businesses and organizations truly valued Diversity of Thought, the need for Rebels at Work would decline significantly. So I spent some time this weekend checking out the latest research on the topic.

The good news is that there is some recent research. The most noteworthy is an MIT study published this fall that examines whether diversity of teams in terms of gender and tenure was associated with 1. team harmony and 2. team productivity (as measured by revenue.) The study doesn't measure diversity of thought per se, but gender differences and varying levels of work experience often are associated with the clash of ideas in the workplace.

The study has some interesting and sometimes counter-intuitive findings. Teams composed of members who were hired at different times did not show lower levels of cooperation, but, according to the researchers, did show significantly lower levels of performance. Teams with higher levels of gender diversity, however, were associated with reduced team harmony, but in this case these teams were also associated with significantly higher levels of performance. (Interestingly, mixed gender teams easily outperformed both all-male and all-female teams.)

The press has popularized the study by reporting that diverse teams are more productive but less happy. But I think the study points to a more nuanced conclusion—the need for managers to develop better techniques for dealing with differences in the workplace, whatever their causes.

The tension that comes with the clash of ideas is a frequent challenge for Rebels at Work. Often, the Rebel is so caught up in the excitement of advancing her ideas that she fails to notice and/or discounts the unhappiness and discomfort building among her teammates. The manager, whose training emphasized the need to build consensus but not how to navigate turbulent whitewater, is often just a bystander as his team blows up. Clearly, there's a lot of work to be done here.

Some preliminary ideas for managers of rebels

"Rethink your default settings." The phrase comes from a report by a UK consultancy on how to increase diversity on boards. I'm using it here to refer to the habits and practices that managers of team rarely question. How do you run your meetings? Whom do you talk to first about an issue? What priorities does your calendar reflect? Examine everything and consider upending most of it. For example, if you have a new influx of team members, let them set the agenda for an upcoming meeting. Give them a chance to share their observations without interruption.

Acknowledge different categories of "expertise" for your team. I've seen many teams where only one type of expertise is recognized and valued. Either you are on expert on how things have always been done—standard operating procedures, or you're here to learn. Sound familiar? But how about having a team discussion on the different types of expertise that could be useful to meeting team goals. Who is most familiar with the new research? Who here understands the growing Hispanic market? Who is on top of new technology? Just having an explicit conversation about the many categories of useful knowledge can be an eye opening experience for team members.

Talk explicitly about individual thinking and work styles. There's any number of free tests on the internet about thinking styles and they are all useful. But recently I've found it to be just as effective to have team members describe "how they think" or "how they solve problems" to each other. Most people know if they are good with detail or if they prefer to play with bigger concepts. I've come to believe that most job performance issues are caused by asking people to do tasks for which they are not well-suited. Forget the job descriptions. Let individuals gravitate to the tasks they do well.

Ask more open-ended questions and tell fewer lies. OK, well maybe managers don't tell lies on purpose. But in their effort to project certainty, they often make pronouncements suffused with an unjustified air of certainty. Monitor the number of declarative sentences you make as a manager and resolve to replace at least a third of them with questions. Here's an example. A team member asks you how the team plans to meet a difficult deadline. Instead of providing your not-so-definitive answer, why not just reflect the question back to the team. "That's a great question. What ideas do you all have." You've now encouraged everyone on your team to speak, including the different thinkers and rebels.

Why You Should Embrace Your Heretics

A great article by Polly LaBarre in Fortune Magazine highlights examples of organizations that realize the need for rebels—including IBM's John Patrick, Kim Spinder, a Dutch Ministry employee whose small rebel action transformed 400+ government offices to collaborate, and our own Carmen Medina of the CIA.

> *"Too many people still work in organizations that resemble the IBM of their grandfather's (or great-grandfather's) day—organizations designed to exert tight control at the expense of autonomy, to maximize compliance over individual expression and discretion. Yet if we want originality and invention, we need to fill our organizations with people who ignore the rules, flout convention, question constantly, and experiment fearlessly. We need the rebels and the troublemakers because, as Apple's Think Different campaign put it, "they change things. They push the human race forward."*

Especially interesting was Seth Godin's view on what it takes to make an organization safe for rebels and heretics: "There's a big difference between religion and faith. Religion is the set of rules created to maximize the chances that you will do what the manager wants you to do. A heretic is someone who has faith but could care less about religion."

Stupid Things Bosses Say!

Rebels at Work exist because organizations and leaders fail sometimes, or maybe more often than that. When we talk to managers and leaders, however, most of them say they sincerely want to encourage new ideas from their workforce. But what they don't comprehend are the unintended consequences of the words they use. Words that bosses think encourage new ideas from their workforce just don't... and sometimes they actually turn off the spigot.

Let's see how you do on the following True-False test. These phrase may or may not encourage team members to share their ideas for improvement.

Do you have any comments?

FALSE. Probably the most common phrase bosses use to end meetings. We've yet to talk to any employee, however, who thought the phrase actually was an invitation for anyone to speak. Usually said after a 50-minute monologue, this question seems more intended to indicate that the meeting has come to an end. Certainly what you get is...crickets.

I have an open door policy.

FALSE. A reliable chestnut for "good bosses" everywhere and yet remarkably ineffective. I'm sure some of you are wondering what could be wrong with having an Open Door policy. Think about where that phrase puts the onus for action—not on the boss, of course, but on the employees. Yes, you can share an idea with me but you have to come into the official Boss Space to share it. The best way for a boss to have an "open door" policy is not to ever mention it, not to make a big deal of it, but simply, through her actions, to demonstrate that she is always approachable. We're reminded of the apocryphal story concerning what St. Francis of Assisi said when asked about the best way to evangelize:

Preach the gospel at all times, and if necessary use Words!

I manage through consensus.

FALSE. Another popular management "best practice" that we take issue with. When you say you value consensus you are of course sending the clear message that you don't like disagreements. Your employees will wonder what standard their concerns or opinion must meet to warrant mentioning. This is not a productive dynamic.

Don't bring me a problem unless you have a solution.

So of course by now the attentive reader knows we think this is FALSE. In fact, we would go so far to say that it is one of the stupidest notions in modern management. When an employee notices something is amiss, he should be encouraged to mention it as quickly as possible. Asking the observer to also provide the solution reinforces the unhealthy view that excellence in organizations is about individual performance. Excellence is more sustainable when it is team-based. An individual who notices a problem should be encouraged to engage his coworkers early on to identify a solution.

So what should bosses say to encourage Rebels at Work. It's actually pretty simple.

What did I get wrong?

What are we missing?

What would you add?

How would you do it differently?

Why don't you take the lead?

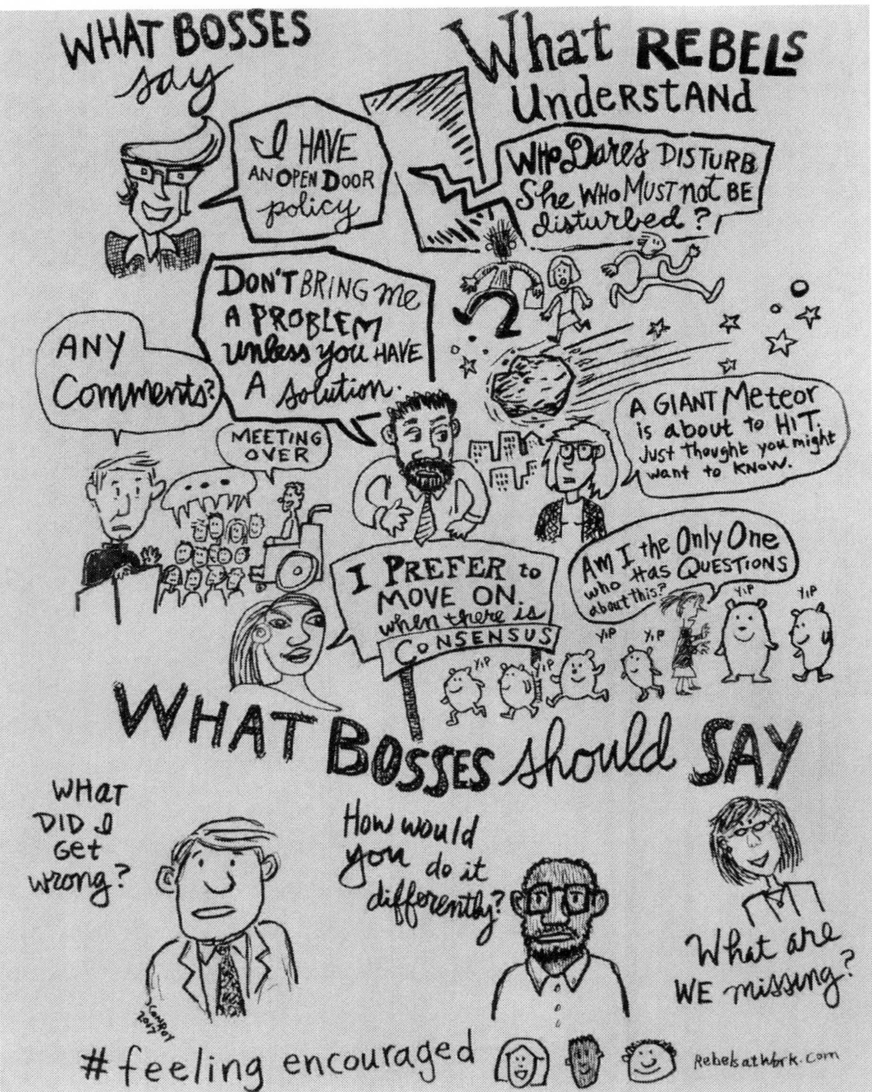

Why Leaders Reject Rebels and Innovative Ideas

When our brain senses that our status is being threatened, our thinking shuts down. We avoid the person or situation making us feel so uncomfortable, and we often stay away from any activity or idea about which we're not confident. Worse, we label the other person as "wrong" so we can be "right."

We don't necessarily do this consciously. It's just our brains' natural response when our status is under attack, say the neuroscientists.

So when Rebels challenge an organization's status quo and executive decisions, leaders' brains go on high-alert. Their decisions, their plans, their position feel threatened and under attack. The neuroscience research says this threat to status activates the same brain regions as physical pain.

The leaders' knee-jerk reaction is often to label the people with the fresh new ideas as troublemakers. Or not having enough experience to really know what they're talking about. And jeez, that kid isn't even a manager, what could she know? (See how put downs can make you feel better and restore your status?)

Guess what this reaction does to people with the fresh ideas that you need to lead? They run for the hills. Maybe they try to approach you or another executive again, but you're likely not to welcome what they have to say. Through words, tone or body language you broadcast the message throughout your organization: your ideas are NOT WELCOME.

And then you wonder why the culture isn't more innovative and creative. Why too few people speak up with substantive comments at meetings. Why it seems like you're the only one with the answers.

Time to get your brain in line and recognize your "threat" triggers so that you can control them — instead of them controlling you.

Who needs to change their ways: leaders or rebels?

Some executives have told me that "rebels and change agents need to learn how business works. You can't just disrupt things and expect everyone to change."

But should the corporate rebels be the ones to have to adapt their style? Or should leaders find ways to better understand how to control *their* threat triggers so that they can create a safe, welcoming climate for new ideas?

To me, this is the responsibility of the leader. All people can benefit from understanding and managing what trips them up. But with the prestige and financial compensation of being a leader comes the responsibility for first and foremost managing oneself. So your head is ready to be in the game of leading.

Humility and reappraising

This is why so many great leaders are humble. Humility reduces the status threat. It puts people at ease talking with you. It clears the leader's mind of emotion so that he or she can really understand what people are saying.

Another way to manage the brain is to reappraise situations that start to trigger your emotions. What's the other person's perspective? What does he want me to understand? What does she want me to do and why? Look at what's being said as data and nothing more.

Economic and competitive threats are relentless, causing their own set of threats and associated behavioral responses. But to succeed companies need new ideas and the best ideas are likely to come from the rebels and mavericks inside your own organization.

As a leader, help those people who can most help you succeed. Even if they make you uncomfortable. Maybe especially because they make you uncomfortable.

Help yourself by seeing challenges to the status quo as possibilities not attacks on your position.

Silence of the Rebels

This week I had an experience that reminded me of just how difficult it is for corporate rebels to speak up.

"Lois, I need to tell you something," she whispered nervously as I walked into the ladies room. Then she quickly searched the stalls to make no one from her management team was there.

"I know why the workshop isn't working," she said with conviction.

Now I was on high alert, having walked into the bathroom frustrated and discouraged about the leadership workshop I was facilitating. The topic was on how to lead meetings so that people have honest conversations and share different points of views. But the energy in the workshop was low and the engagement almost non-existent. Was it the material? Was I having an off day? Do these people not have meetings? Could I turn this around after the break or should I just end it and put all of us out of our misery?

"It's trust," she whispered. "I'm fairly new here and can see the problem. But no one sees it because they confuse friendliness with trust. I have to go. Please, don't tell anyone I told you this."

Wow. Having worked with this client before I never would have thought that trust was an issue. They are such nice people.

Organizational silence = shutting down ideas

After the break I started the session with "organizational silence" research from NYU Professor Elizabeth Wolfe Morrison.

"Perhaps what's really at play here is nothing about how to lead meetings.

It's about your organization. Meetings simply mirror the culture. In most organizations leaders don't like negative feedback and consciously and subconsciously believe that they know more than the rank and file. These beliefs silence people from speaking up. We never hear what we need to hear. What does that do to a business?"

Radio silence.

Then one brave young man raised his hand. "Yes, it feels kind of unsafe to say anything at our meetings. I don't get the sense that people really want to hear my point of view."

Then people started talking. After two and a half hours we were having the real conversation.

"A troubling aspect of the dynamics that create and maintain silence is that they are hidden from view and often unrecognized" says Professor Morrison. "Management may see that employees are not engaged, but may assume that it is because they are self-interested or not motivated."

How to break the silence? Professor Morrison offers these suggestions:

Don't shoot the messenger: In terms of prevention, managers must work hard to counteract the natural human tendency to avoid negative feedback. They must not only seek out honest feedback, on a regular basis, they must also be careful to not "shoot the messenger" when they receive bad news.

Create a safe climate: Managers must also work hard to build an open and trusting climate within their organizations, one in which employees know that their input is valued and that it is safe to speak up.

Really want to hear it: If employees sense that those above them do not want to hear about potential problems and issues of concern, they will not talk about them. Managers must recognize this dynamic and convince employees that they do want input.

Replace top managers: One way to create such a change (of open communication) is to bring in new top managers. This will not only enable the organization to break from its past, but will signal to employees that there is a commitment to changing the status quo.

There are no solutions, only practice

There is no easy way for leaders to create safe corporate cultures. There are no simple solutions for being the corporate rebel who raises issues no one really wants to hear, despite their value.

Learning to create safe corporate cultures and raising difficult issues are lifelong practices. We're never done.

The Lazy Manager

When I was but a pup, still going to graduate school, a professor came to me and said:

"Carmen I can tell that you're going to be a manager some day." (This came as quite a shock to me!) "And I have only one piece of advice for you."

"What's that, Dr. Stearman?" (His name was William Stearman and Wikipedia tells me he is still alive. I always considered him a pro's pro in the national security realm.)

"Be lazy!"

Well that wasn't what I was expecting to hear and it took me years, if not decades, to understand what he was getting at. But as my own work style developed, I found that I— and more importantly others—had more success when I delegated, perhaps you might even say abdicated, and just let others do what they did well. Not fake delegation when you ask someone to handle a task and then hover around pressing them to get it done at **your pace**, not theirs. That's not delegating; instead it's a type of manipulation that comes second nature to many.

Nope, when a manager is effectively delegating and appropriately lazy, she begins to entertain doubts as to whether she's needed at all on a work team. That's the indicator that you're lazy enough.

I reflected back on Dr. Stearman's advice recently upon reading this article about how procrastination is an effective management technique. The author contends that managers who are over-eager to answer employee questions and help them solve problems are getting in the way of their development. The author urges managers to procrastinate more, delay in being helpful. Dr. Stearman would have gotten right to the point: Be Lazy!

This discussion also gives me an opportunity to share a clip from my favorite movie about teams and management, ***Galaxy Quest.*** Ah yes, you may only know this movie as a humorous send-up of the Star Trek/Wars genre. But I have long wanted to organize a leadership seminar around the lessons of ***Galaxy Quest***. In the movie, a group of aliens intercepts the transmissions of the Planet Earth television show Galaxy Quest and are so inspired by the brave crew that they successfully replicate the TV show's technology. Mayhem ensues when the aliens, unable to deploy the technology effectively against their evil enemies, "kidnap" the crew—now unemployed actors doing the "trekkie" convention circuit—to come help them fight the war.

The lessons in the movie for organizations are many. Tim Allen plays the egotistical Captain Kirk character, and his fellow actors hate him. They only begin to succeed when they start operating as a team by respecting each other's contributions. We also learn about the importance of emotional resonance and how "being corny" can be an effective quality for leaders.

The clip illustrates the value of procrastination/laziness by a manager. Tech Sergeant Chen, played by Tony Shalhoub, has been asked by the aliens to troubleshoot a problem with their reactor. Of course, Chen don't know nothing about beryllium reactors, but, by asking open-ended questions, he prompts the crew to solve the problem themselves. (If you ***Galaxy Quest*** devotees aren't familiar with this scene, that's because it didn't make the final cut of the movie. But it should have!)

EMBRACE MESSINESS

Get Things Under Control

"The Cardinals are tired of reading about financial corruption, sexual improprieties and infighting at the Vatican. They want a Pope who can get things under control," explained Father Thomas Reese to Tom Ashbrook on his NPR "On Point" radio show today.

Calls to "get things under control" leave no hope for control.

Whether it's trying to control clergy in the Catholic Church, parents angry over school policies, or customers tweeting unfavorable product reviews, there is no control.

When I hear "get things under control" I know it's a situation that can only be addressed by getting at root cause issues. It's not a "handling" or crisis communications issue, it's a systemic issue requiring that the real problems be addressed.

No new Pope can get the Catholic Church "under control" without addressing some deep seated issues around child sex abuse.

No business leader can get customers under control if customers hate the products or customer service.

No school official can get parents under control if they feel their children are not being served.

No politician can get voters under control if they believe the politician is more interested in getting elected than representing their views.

No good can come from trying to control.

The Stability Trap

Given my long career at the CIA, I still read widely on international relations and politics. One of the most interesting articles I've read in some time just appeared in Foreign Affairs—The Calm Before the Storm—Why Volatility Signals Stability, and Vice Versa.

Trying to figure out when and how a society becomes unstable is the bread and butter work of a political analyst in the Intelligence Community. Nassim Taleb's and Greg Treverton's article is wonderfully contrarian, arguing that in fact the most stable societies have a history of healthy volatility in their recent past.

Reflecting on my own career, I can remember many countries that I knew were going to implode at any moment, and yet somehow never did. And when there was a surprise—or, in other words, an intelligence failure—it was often because a pillar of the international community had suddenly—or so we thought—gone all wobbly on us.

And then I wondered whether this nifty piece of analysis could have broader implications.

Wait a Minute!

Could this apply to companies as well? Could it in fact be the case that the best indicator of an organization's future stability is not past stability but moderate volatility in the relatively recent past?

Rebels at Work know that one of the main reasons why their ideas don't get a fair hearing is because most management teams prefer, indeed they crave, stability.

My experience in government and the private sector is that one of the real reasons people avoid change is because they dislike disruption. Changing an organization is like staying in your house when you're remodeling your kitchen. It's messy and uncomfortable. As a result, people in an organization often will agree that the future end state is much preferable to the Status Quo, but nevertheless get grumpy at the thought of any disruption of their daily routines.

Organizations and managers need to rethink this aversion to messiness, to moderate volatility. And one of the best ways for a company to inject a healthy dose of ideational volatility into its operations is to be more tolerant, perhaps even welcoming, of its rebels, mavericks, and heretics.

I can promise you that we rebels are very good at stirring things up if you just let us. Injecting new ideas into the tired debate about next year's strategic direction would make all organizations stronger. Encouraging dissent from the prevailing wisdom in organizations is analogous to the "political variability" that characterizes countries that enjoy genuine political stability. As Taleb and Treverton point out, decentralization and political changeability makes countries stronger; authoritarian rule tends to only make them brittle.

Many companies and organizations today are brittle. They look strong but that strength is untested. The absence of diversity in their strategy and tactics leaves them vulnerable to any changes in the environment they fail to anticipate. Rebels at Work can serve as the anticipation engine of your organization.

But only if you let them!

Smooth and Easy DOESN'T Cut It!

The LinkedIn Conversation on our post Stupid Things Bosses Say! led to a robust series of comments worth summarizing here. The bottom line is reflected in the title: the tendency of organizations to reward the "smooth leadership style" is detrimental to diversity of thought, discourages everyone from offering potentially helpful suggestions and/or dissents, and leads to lowest common denominator outcomes.

One reader asked whether there is a magic potion leaders can take to become more welcoming to different opinions. Our answer: there is no magic potion and the very idea that there could be a magic potion is part of the problem. But there is an insidious dynamic in most workplaces that—if removed—would make it easier for managers to welcome healthy debate on their teams.

Organizations need to stop grading leaders on how "smoothly" their operations run. You usually don't get diversity of opinions when teams run "smoothly." And yet most organizations I'm familiar with reward managers who run "tight ships." "You never hear about any problems from her team." goes the familiar refrain. "She must be a good manager!"

Maybe not. When decisions are made quickly, it may very well mean that dissent is not tolerated or even suppressed. Feisty teams aren't ever going to be quiet teams.

And that leads to another situation.. Once different opinions are allowed to surface, meetings become crunchier and, even when everyone has the best of intentions, some ruffling of feathers will occur. Most managers don't know how to deal with "diversity tension." And no one really bothers to teach them. In fact leadership and management training focuses instead on alpha capabilities such as vision and decision-making. Instead we need to learn how to empower employees who disagree with us and how to tell when you the manager is dead wrong.

Sounds pretty radical, right?

But at Rebels at Work, we like radical. We like texture and crunchiness.

And we don't mind it when it's rough and hard!

Innovation is the Opposite of Policy

Lois Kelly and I are regularly amazed and humbled by the resonance that Rebels at Work continues to have. And just when we think there aren't any new wrinkles out there for us to share, we come across a new voice.

Daniel Hulter is in the US Air Force. He is writing about innovation on LinkedIn. And he shared a piece recently that made a wonderful and necessary distinction between innovation as the glamorous endeavors of Mavericks and the almost routine actions of individuals who figure out the right thing to do in any given situation. Like the individual in a bureaucracy who has the wisdom to see that a policy, written forty years ago by individuals perhaps no longer on this mortal coil, cannot be followed in a particular human situation.

Hulter has the hunch—and we agree—that if organizations worried more about encouraging the latter and less about their flagship innovation projects, they would improve just as quickly with less *sturm und drang.*

A simple and meaningful definition of Innovation is the Opposite of Policy.

Policy incorporates what the past has told us about the best way to do something—and let me just say that the "best way" incorporates a whole set of assumptions that merit examination. For example, organizations often think that smooth operations are the **BEST** operations; the desire for smoothness, however, can trample over other good things such as diversity of thought and trying out new ideas.

But let me add a qualifier. Not all policies are bad and not all innovation is good.

Amy from Minneapolis (not her real name) wrote me to complain that it's not a good thing when employees in a large organization ignore security policies and thus open themselves to malicious hacking. Some policies are worth having and some innovations are just stupid. It is an annoying fact of life that to navigate it successfully you must learn to maneuver through the grey. Shades of grey are difficult to distinguish from black or white. What I thought was a simple matter turns out more nuanced. That's why you need allies, disagreeable givers, a wild pack, and, yes, even opponents to help you see.

Change is Hard, but Judging Change Initiatives is Even Harder

The tale of the goddess Athena, springing fully formed (and fully armed!!) from the forehead of Zeus is one of the great stories of Greek mythology, although perhaps it is more accurate to say of Mediterranean basin mythology given that people living there in ancient times shared many of the same myths.

The story is quite colorful, as it actually has Zeus swallowing Athena's mother who busily kept forming Athena inside Zeus until she was ready to be launched—a perfect creation. (Here is the Wikipedia version of the tale.)

But unlike the emergence of Athena, everything we have around us in society, in biology, in organizations is the result of a long, often messy, incremental process. (Another word for that is evolution, but I don't want to get involved in an ideological fracas just yet—although I do hope to tackle the perils of ideology at some point.)

None of our current institutions, whether it be the Department of Transportation or the Cable Television System or marriage or astronomy, emerged fully and intelligently formed out of some brilliant individual's forehead.

No, they usually began as half-baked ideas and that took turns and detours not anticipated by their originators and early supporters. And, this is the important point, we shouldn't want it any other way. For only through a process that allows a "thing" to react to the environment around it, change and adapt, can we produce organizations, processes, customs, and institutions that actually work, deliver most of their promise, and are organically one with their environments.

But if you're an advocate of a Change Initiative for an organization or a group, the first thing you hear from anyone you brief is: "Well, how is the whole thing going to work?" The only honest answer to that question is "I don't really know. We'll have to monitor that carefully." Although by so admitting you might as well just slink back to the advanced methods lab from whence you came.

The status quo may have had a 50-year development process with abundant beautiful messiness, but if you as the Change Advocate can't present the future operating environment as a beautiful schematic in a series of PowerPoint slides, with some vaguely inspirational and symmetrical logo in the corner, then you're as doomed as doomed can be.

This then becomes a real leadership moment for a Federal Government or any other senior executive. Don't be the executive whose expectations for neat and orderly change force your enthusiastic future-thinkers to become hypocrites and to package their proposals in Power-pointless slide decks. Because if you demand certainty, you not only will buy into intellectual fraud, you will also eventually tear the heart out of your change champions.

Approach change for what it is—the normal course adjustment process that keeps your organization alive.

RELATING TO REBELS

Trust is a Muscle

"How do I know when I can trust a Rebel at Work?"

We often get asked this question. A manager or team leader hears Lois or I present, agrees with our message that the people who work for him often have solutions for the team's problems or can identify new opportunities, but double clutches at the point of empowerment. Can I trust her?

In this instance, the manager is using the word trust to mean: Can I rely upon her to execute successfully? Can I be completely confident? Admittedly that is one of the dictionary meanings of the word. But there's another sense of trust that is more relevant to the manager/rebel relationship.

To quote from a short paper prepared about ten years ago for the Canadian Department of Defense by Dr. Barbara Adams:

> *A trust judgement... is characterized by a specific lack of information, and by the need to take a "leap of faith" from what is known to what is unknown.*

Trust, according to Dr. Adams, is only operational in situations with risk. But when managers want to know when they can TRUST rebels at work, what they really want to know is how can they make sure that their empowerment of a rebel is risk-free.

Which is the wrong expectation!! Fundamentally, trust is a judgment call.

The leader is making a decision even in the absence of some data—such as previous experience with an individual in a similar circumstance. But the leader can reason that the risk is justified by the potential gain. And that potential gain is not just measured by whether the idea works or not.

When a leader trusts an employee with a new initiative, they not only send a signal to that individual but to the rest of the team that it's not just experience that matters; new ideas have value too.

In fact, it's kind of circular.

The only way to determine whether you can trust a Rebel at Work is by trusting one. Trust is a muscle. It benefits from being used. The first time you provide space for team members to work on their new ideas you can't be sure how it will turn out. But by doing so you gain experience that will inform your next trust moment and the expectations of your team.

At some point, particularly if you rarely use your trust muscles, one of your decisions will misfire. (No pain, no gain!) And you will have learned something important about the individuals involved, including yourself. As Dr. Adams notes, "a trust decision typically involves the formation of an impression about another person rather than merely making an estimate with respect to a discrete and specific task." Trust is an investment in your team and an engagement with them as individuals.

The only way to strengthen it is by using it!

Techniques for Throwing Corporate Rebels Under the Bus

Managers are so sloppy when it comes to throwing corporate rebels under the bus.

Usually they are so damn angry with the employee that they botch their technique.

They are irrationally rough, their aim is imprecise and messy, and they end up running over the body with such force that it causes more damage to the employee than they intended. But it does seem a relief to have gotten rid of *that* problem.

Few think about an important follow-through skill: contact with the other employees still on the bus. Just as a baseball pitcher throws a pitch and then needs to be prepared to field the hit, you can't just throw someone under the bus. You need to be ready for what comes next.

Alas, most get sloppy here. Despite carefully throwing someone under the bus at discrete places or times, or telling employees that the person *asked* to get off the bus or jumped out of the bus, annoying glitches happen.

Employees on the bus are shaken up when the bus unexpectedly hits and runs over something strange, like their colleague. They get scared and distracted from work; many update their resumes.

Then they see their ex-colleague outside of work, bruised, angry and victimized, stumbling around in disbelief. The water cooler gossip goes wild, people wonder aloud why bosses throw people under the bus, and they secretly fear it could happen to them.

What a mess. Not even HR does a good job cleaning it up. For being so precise with financial spreadsheets and quality standards, why can 't managers be better at throwing employees under the bus?

Why managers throw employees under the bus

First, let's review reasons why they throw corporate rebels under the bus:

1. They are irate that the employee **questioned their decisions in a public forum.** How dare they! Being humiliated by that subordinate? I'm in charge, goddammit.

2. The employee has been meeting with people in the company to **stir up ideas and support around an area that is not one of your five key strategic imperatives.** Who gave them permission to do that? Why do they think they are entitled to be creating new strategies outside the standard chain of command? Bet their parents coddled them. Probably were on those sports teams where *every* kid gets a trophy.

3. Fairly new to the company, the employee **just doesn't get how things work.** They seem to miss all the obvious social signals and are getting on people's nerves. Can't they see that they're suppose to informally socialize new ideas before bringing them up in monthly staff meetings? What's with

the talk, talk, talk with the junior people? And strolling into the office at 9:30? Geez. Do I have to explain how everything works around here?

4. **They are upsetting *your* boss** and to save face with the big cheese, you need to act decisively and swiftly to eliminate the problem and calm your boss down. Like having an odd-looking mole removed from your face before it develops into full-blown skin cancer. I'm not going to jeopardize *my career* over someone making waves. She did bring some fresh thinking and energy we could sorely use around here, but after finally making it to senior vice president I'm not going to jeopardize my career.

Those in category #4 are the sloppiest at throwing people under the bus, yet seem to do it more often, too. When insecurities twist a person in knots, they get reckless and irrational. Despite throwing more people under the bus than most managers, they really make a mess at it. Insecurity is a killer.

Improving your skills at throwing rebels under the bus

So how to improve your skills in throwing corporate rebels under the bus?

Well, before even getting to those skills I'd suggest that first you might want to consider a brush up course in bus driving.

If you get better at focusing on your destination and getting the right people on your bus, you might not have to throw anyone off or under the bus. The focus will also help avoid distractions when employees on the bus get rowdy or restless, or someone starts hogging everyone's attention even when you've told him to stay in his seat.

The refresher course will remind you to pay attention when employees on the bus yell at you from the back of the bus. They probably aren't criticizing your driving. It may be that they see a giant pothole ahead, or know a great short cut, or even want to drive for a while so you can get some rest for what you all know is a challenging journey.

And if your boss calls demanding an explanation about why you're taking a different route than planned, drivers ed will teach you to stay calm and explain to you boss that several employees know this territory well and saw a better way to get to the destination. Sure he may fume and make threats. But your employees on the bus are with you, ready to fix the flats, pump gas in the rain, figure out ways around detours.

Who is going to go the extra mile for you? Them, or the boss?

Drive safely.

Like a Rebel Boss

My son is about to turn 20 and I'm so proud of him. Prouder still of me.

I didn't throw objects, nag incessantly, take away privileges, drone on about accountability and responsibility, or yell and scream like a raving maniac during those teen years. (Well, except for that one freak out. More on that in a minute.)

Reflecting on those years I realize that becoming a good boss of Rebels can help you become a better parent. Especially during the teenage years.

There are many good reasons to be a good boss of those rebels and mavericks who, like teenagers, think current policies and approaches are stupid and want to change everything. If you help Rebels, they'll go to the mat for your organization and you'll likely get a promotion, score a big bonus, look good with the suits on the executive floor, and be the person everyone in the company wants to work for.

But the real reason to coach rebels like a rock star is to train yourself for those teenage years. If you have teenagers or have made it through, you likely know what I'm talking about. If you don't yet have teenage children, take this advice and thank me later.

Like the rebels who work for us, we love our teenagers' fresh thinking, their creativity, their intolerance for school and societal rules that just don't make sense, and their willingness to do something about those stupid rules. They are so bold, vibrant and confident that it can take our breath away. We want to be them.

And yet they make us crazy when they skirt the rules, do dumb things without understanding the bigger context, let their emotions run wild, and screw up so badly that we have to have one of those dreaded meetings with the principle or the CEO where no one really knows what to say except, "Talk to her. Try to keep him in line. I know she's basically a good student/employee. One last thing — let's not let this happen again." You walk away feeling like a reprimanded teenager.

Better for rebels, better for teenagers

So what helps us help Rebels at work – and, in turn, helps us help our teenagers at home?

When we coach rebels and help them learn how to navigate within existing structures however screwed up they may be, they develop capacities for being effective, meaningful employees. If we simply insist they follow the rules, they just get angrier and more frustrated. Saying, "the rules are the rules" to idea people at work and creative kids at home is like talking in a different language. Like a language with all guttural, ugly sounds. They just hear the hard edges and look at the spit coming out of our mouths and think, "How pathetic."

I tried, not always successfully, to remark more on what my teenage son was doing well than on what he should be doing differently or better. I'd ask him what was working in school or share my work challenges and ask him what he thought might be the best approach. I valued his opinions because I knew they would be honest, frank and fresh. Not the usual blah-blah responses.

Rebels at work also provide this freshness. Don't miss out on these perspectives. They're foreign, like a teenager's, but with more wisdom.

Conversations with rebels, like teens, can't be superficial or disingenuous. They'll tune you out, and you'll miss out.

What worries you? What else do you think is possible? What are we kidding ourselves about? What might happen if we...

Questions teach, both them and us.

Rebels and teens know a lot. They think a lot. And they'll help you gain new perspectives. Their ideas might make you feel uncomfortable. OK, they will make you feel uncomfortable. But that's how we learn, right?

By hearing and considering their views, we build trust, love, mutuality, togetherness, bonding. Most importantly, we build their capacity to consider other views and learn how to disagree without being a jerk. To be able to talk about ideas where no one is right or wrong. To feel safe enough to disagree and still feel safe and valued as part of the family or as part of the organization.

Freak out!

As long as they don't steal your credit card to buy World of Warcraft add-ons.

This is where the freak out happened.

My son and I had had several conversations about getting the gaming thing under control. So when I opened my card statement and saw several different $25 charges from Blizzard Entertainment, I went nuts.

He came home from school all cheerful and I started screaming, channeling an Irish banshee, waving my credit card bill. I was maniacal, and one scary woman. To finish off my tantrum I slammed the front door, got in the car, and drove off leaving my son at home alone for several hours.

When I finally came home, he had written a letter to me, not only apologizing but also explaining how he would pay me back and, much more importantly, how he was going to cure the burgeoning World of Warcraft addiction. "That I've disappointed you is the worse thing of all," he wrote.

He had a plan that was far better than anything that I could have constructed. He beat himself up harder than I ever would or could.

From having been the boss of rebels, I guess I knew that he would figure out a way forward that was more insightful and effective than anything I could imagine.

Because we had a relationship built on honesty and mutual caring, I knew we would recover. No one had to win or lose.

I love that boy, who I now have to call a man. He's creative, passionate, dedicated, often unrealistic in setting goals, curious, and sometimes self-absorbed when he's in the flow of a project.

Like a rebel. Like the best people who ever worked in my organizations.

So if you have a rebel working for you, rejoice! Coach, ask questions, let go of control while setting some boundaries, and make it safe to talk about the tough stuff.

You're going to love the teenage years.

About the Authors

Carmen Medina's personal motto is that Optimism is the Greatest Act of Rebellion. To prove her point, she spent 32 years as a heretic at CIA. Since retiring, she's devoted most of her energy to helping other optimists who want to make work an uplifting experience for all.

Lois Kelly worked in digital marketing and strategic communications for Fortune 500 companies. She's certified in Positive Psychology, happiest when creating art, and devoted to helping people find more meaning and moments of joy in their work.

Social Media Links

Website: https://www.rebelsatwork.com/

Facebook: https://www.facebook.com/RebelsatWork/

Twitter: https://twitter.com/rebelsatwork

Instagram: https://www.instagram.com/rebelsatwork/

Made in the USA
Middletown, DE
20 June 2020

10546557R00194